COACHING
FOOTBALL'S
DOUBLE SLOT ATTACK

Larry Strauch

Parker Publishing Company, Inc.
West Nyack, New York

© 1979 *by*

Parker Publishing Company, Inc.

West Nyack, New York

Library of Congress Cataloging in Publication Data

Strauch, Larry
   Coaching football's double slot attack.

   Includes index.
   1. Football--Offense. 2. Football coaching.
I. Title.
GV951.S85   796.33'22   78-18515
ISBN 0-13-139337-5

Printed in the United States of America

DEDICATION

To my parents, Martin and Jean Strauch, for their infinite patience and encouragement. Without them I would not have experienced such a rewarding and successful career.

Also, to my two brothers, Paul and Phil, for their strong support throughout my coaching experience.

OFFENSIVE SUCCESS WITH THE DOUBLE SLOT —
HOW THIS BOOK WILL HELP YOU

The Double Slot is a very flexible offensive system that incorporates a number of play schemes and offensive philosophies. This book includes a comprehensive survey of how the Double Slot achieves this degree of flexibility. The material and play schemes are presented so that you may select various plays to the extent you desire. You may want to run only selected plays from the entire offense or develop a total commitment to the Double Slot attack.

The formation is a compilation of numerous offensive play types adapted to a single formation. Because of these adaptations the offense is unique. Included in the attack is the power running game derived from the Single Wing and Wing T. Modern trends in the option game are also presented. The passing game adapts many of the trends in the current Pro styles.

Simple line blocking assignments are covered with plays diagrammed against basic common defensive fronts. These various defenses include the 5-2 and 4-3 as 7-man fronts, and the 4-4 and 5-3 as 8-man alignments. All blocking schemes are illustrated against these various defenses and some of the more frequent stunts executed off them. With the presentation of each play are the key coaching points that assist you with the implementation of the offense. In several situations supportive diagrams provide extra emphasis regarding a particular technique.

Chapter 1 deals primarily with the theory of the Double Slot and the general problems that it creates for the defense. Included also are the coaching points for the formation alignment, the huddle designation and the naming of the selected play. Hole numbering systems and the snap count are also dealt with. Chapter 1 concludes with a presentation of blocking rules and how various defensive structures are broken down by numbering.

Chapters 2 and 3 deal primarily with the running game as it develops from the quick dive to the fullback. Heavy emphasis is placed on the option attack as this series is perhaps the most effective from the Double Slot formation. Included in the option game are both the double and triple variations along with the various problems that the offense will encounter. Chapter 3 presents traps and power off-tackle plays derived from the fullback dive action. All plays are supported with diagrams, assignments, individual techniques and key coaching points.

The running game is further developed and dealt with in Chapters 4, 5 and 6. In Chapter 4 plays that are derived directly from the Single Wing and Wing T offenses are discussed. Chapter 5 deals once more with the option game with emphasis on the diversity of the option play types. Emphasis is placed on the strategical application of the option for a given number of tactical situations. Chapter 6 deals with the Belly play to the fullback. Included are the Outside Belly, Counters, Belly Options; a counter play with the tackle trapping is included with the intention of having it function as a complementary play to the counter game.

Chapter 7 offers a number of play actions that are not series oriented and are classified more as special plays. Included is the End Around from both the split end and tight end formation alignments. The Power Sweep is also presented with a halfback reverse off this action as a special feature.

Chapters 8 and 9 concentrate on the throwing game. This phase of the offense receives as much emphasis as the option and is extremely effective when utilized from the Double Slot formation. Chapter 8 deals with pass routes and play-calling methods with emphasis placed on key coaching points. Various launch areas and pass actions are discussed. You are provided with an overview of defensive secondary looks and adjustments that the offense will encounter when developing its pass strategy. Chapter 9 deals with a complete protection blocking system. Individual techniques and assignments are provided with extra coaching points on how to coordinate and execute various protection patterns. Both the offensive line and backfield are covered with emphasis being placed on coordinating the entire protection scheme.

The Sprint Out pass game is presented in Chapter 10. One, 2 and 3-man patterns and strategies are covered. Included also is Throwback action with a variety of selected pass patterns illustrated.

Chapter 11 features the dropback game. Again 2 and 3-man strategies are covered. Presented also are selected patterns that are directed to both the strong and weak sides of the offensive formations. Included are "flare control" techniques as well as various methods in "reading" coverages before and after the ball is put into play.

Play action and Screen passes are featured in Chapter 12. Running actions include the Veer, Slant, Buck, Belly and various option maneuvers. Also covered are bootleg and "special" passes that feature the halfback as the passer. Dropback screens, quick screens and play action screens are all discussed.

The *Double Slot* is a guide to coaches seeking an offense to supplement their own style of attack.

Keep in mind that if you use the offense in its entirety or as a supplement to your own, be very selective in the plays that you use. Because of the amount of plays contained in this book, it would be difficult at best for a coaching staff and team to master them all. As a result only a few plays should be chosen and developed. For example, if you are option oriented then select those running (and passing) plays that best fit within the framework of your offensive philosophy. Perhaps to the Wing T coach the Buck series of plays are so closely tied in (practically the same) with that offense that they may serve as an interesting supplement. Should you choose to develop the entire offense within your system, only a few given plays can be run effectively in a given game. Only a small number of plays should be practiced during the preparation time of game week. This small number should be chosen as to their potential effectiveness against the style of defensive play of the upcoming opponent.

                                                             Larry Strauch

Contents

1 Developing an Effective Play Calling System **15**

How the Double Slot Creates Problems for the Defense   15
Formations   16
Motion Types   20
Huddle   23
Naming the Play   24
Line Blocking Rules   26

2 Coaching the Double Slot Veer Series·............................... **33**

Fullback Veer   33
Double Option   38
Triple Option   43

3 Coaching Double Slot Complementary Veer Plays **49**

Halfback Slant   49
Running the Slant Play with Triple Blocking   54
End Option   57

4 Coaching the Double Slot Buck Series **61**

Fullback Buck Dive   62
Fullback Buck Trap   65
Buck Off-Tackle   68
Buck Sweep   72
Bootleg Sweep (Quarterback Sweep)   75

5 Coaching Special Double Slot Option Plays **77**

Straight Option   77
Fullback Option   79

6 Coaching the Double Slot Belly Series **89**

Outside Belly   90
Belly Option   93
Belly Handback Trap   93
Belly Counter   94
Counter Tackle Trap   97

7 Coaching Complementary Double Slot Running Plays **103**

End Around   103
Tight End Sweep   108
Power Sweep   111
Bootleg by the Quarterback   112
Halfback Reverse Off the Power Sweep   113

**8 Developing Pass Play Calling and Summary of
Secondary Coverages** **117**

Release Techniques by Receivers   117
Basic Pass Patterns for Receivers   118
Survey of Defensive Secondary Coverages Against the
Double Slot   124

9 Establishing the Double Slot Pass Actions **137**

Basic Pass Actions   137
Blocking Assignments and Techniques   142
Team Protection Techniques   151

10 Coaching the Double Slot Sprint Out Pass Game **153**

One-Man Patterns   154
Two-Man Patterns   156

Three Man Pass Combinations   158
Semi-Sprint Action   160
Throwback Strategy from the Sprint Pass Game   163
Throwback Action Against 4-Deep Secondaries   167

11 Coaching the Double Slot Dropback Pass Game **171**

Strong Side Pass Game   171
Flare Control   175
Three-Man Patterns   178
Weak Side Dropback Passes   183

12 Coaching Double Slot Play Action and Screen Passes **189**

Veer Action Passes   190
Slant Action Passes   197
Belly Action Passes   200
Buck Action Passes   201
Lead Action Passes   202
Bootlegs   206
Special Passes   208
Screen Passes   211

Index **219**

COACHING

FOOTBALL'S

DOUBLE SLOT ATTACK

1

Developing an Effective Play Calling System

The basic Double Slot formation is illustrated in diagram 1-1. Featured in the alignment are two split ends. Two halfbacks are positioned near the line, each is 1 yard outside the offensive tackle and 1 yard off the line of scrimmage. The backfield alignment features only a single set back, who sets up directly behind the quarterback. Formation variations will be presented later but all alignments feature the backfield positions as just outlined.

HOW THE DOUBLE SLOT
CREATES PROBLEMS FOR THE DEFENSE

There are a number of important effects that the Double Slot achieves by its initial alignment. The problems confronting the defense are presented in 5 basic areas.

First, the Double Slot spreads out the defense. This is based on the concept that the fewer people involved in a football play, the greater the advantage to the offense. When the action is reduced to a 1 on 1 situation the offense should win almost every time. No defender can stand up against a blocker 1 on 1 when a back has any running room. (This concept is supported in the presentation of the option game.) No pass defender can cover a receiver consistently 1-on-1 if both athletes have the same speed. No tackler can consistently stop a ball carrier 1 on 1 in the open field. By its initial alignment the Double Slot starts to break down the defense to this desirable 1 on 1 situation. The complete breakdown occurs during the actual play action.

Second and directly related to the reduction of the play action to a 1-on-1 ratio, is the ability of the Double Slot to control defensive pursuit. It is essential, for a defense to be successful, that it outnumber the offense at the given point of attack. The alignment spreads the defense to a point where it loses its physical and emotional advantages developed by pursuit. Successful defense is numbers, and the Double Slot does best by spreading defenders so that they may not gain a numbers advantage at a given point of attack. The defense, should it over-pursue, is left vulnerable to attacks by counter and reverse plays. Various play schemes discourage unbalanced defenses and are designed to exploit any weak areas apparent in unbalanced defensive alignments.

Third, by its initial deployment the Double Slot is considered primarily as a passing set. This is attributed to the fact that no less than 4 potential receivers are aligned near the line of scrimmage for a quick release into the defensive secondary. As a result the defense is more pass conscious when facing·this formation. Use of a variety of backfield maneuvers allows the development of a surprisingly effective running game as a direct result of the pass threat.

Fourth, the release of the ends and maneuvers by the halfbacks open areas in the defense to run wide with sweeps and option plays. Utilization of formation variations and motion threatens the defense with inside running plays such as the power off-tackle, traps, counters and the basic fullback veer.

Fifth, ultimately the threat of run or pass at the snap forces the defensive players to become conscious of the "big play" taking place in their areas. The combination of the initial pass threats and the effective running game, forces the defense to defend the field in width and depth at the snap. Each action complements another; runs set up the pass and passes set up the run. The Double Slot attacks deep zones, flat area runs at the perimeter and runs inside, and as a result a concept of completeness is achieved. This concept is based on the idea that the defense is forced to defend in completeness, that is, the width and depth of the field when the ball is snapped.

FORMATIONS

Three formations will be utilized in the Double Slot attack. Diagram 1-1 illustrated the standard Double Slot formation. This alignment features two split ends. Against a 3 deep secondary these ends will use a maximum split. If the ball is in the middle of the field, the ends will take a split of 15 yards from the tackle. Should the ball be on a hash mark, the

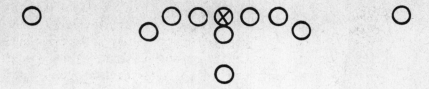

Diagram 1-1

end to the wide side of the field will align on the opposite hash mark. The short side end will line up not closer than 7 yards into the sideline. Diagram 1-2 shows the ball on the hash mark and the split end lining up on the opposite hash. Diagram 1-3 shows another situation where the ball is 3 yards inside the hash mark. The wide side end lines up beyond the opposite hash mark but not closer than 7 yards into the sideline. The reason for the seven yard boundary is that it still leaves enough room for the receivers to run "out" patterns and not allow the defense to use the sideline as a twelfth man that effectively.

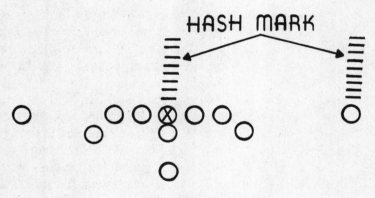

Diagram 1-2

Against a 4-deep secondary the end should split 12 yards from the tackle and again not closer than 7 yards into the sideline. The reason for the shorter split is to threaten invert rotation by the secondary with a screen block by the wide receivers. Also more lateral area must be covered by the defensive back assigned to the outside 1/3 area. Diagram 1-4 shows an inverting secondary on flow and the threat that a 12 yard split by the end creates. If the split end were wider the screen block threat would not be effective and the defense would run that safety on invert action all day either attacking the runs (options and sweeps, etc.) or passes (taking the halfback in the flat).

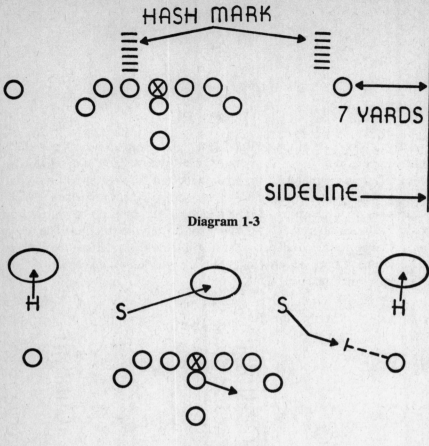

Diagram 1-3

Diagram 1-4

In the basic Double Slot formation the halfbacks align 1 yard outside the tackle and 1 yard off the line of scrimmage. The split from the tackle may be a little tighter against a "gap" defense, where the halfback is included into the blocking scheme.

Generally the interior line splits will adhere to the following guidelines. Adjustments against "gap" defenses will be discussed during the presentation of individual plays.

Guard-Center—2 feet.
Guard-Tackle—3 feet.
Halfback-Tackle—3 feet.

Two other formations are utilized, both featuring the use of a tight end. The first variation retains the split end to one side (he continues to

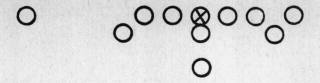

Diagram 1-5

use his hash mark split relationship) and sets an end tight to the opposite side. The tight end aligns 4 feet from the tackle with the halfback still lining up 1 yard outside the tackle and 1 yard off the ball. This forms a tight slot to one side. Diagram 1-5 shows this tight slot alignment. This formation is named in the huddle as "Tight Slot Right" or "Tight Slot Left" and automatically designates the use of a tight end. Generally this formation achieves a balance of opening up the defense to the split end side, while adding an additional blocker to the opposite side. The position of the tight end enhances the development of power running plays (and play action passes) to this side.

The second variation features two tight ends and is used for short yardage and sometimes on the goal line. Here the defense is compressed and the offense desires a maximum blocking effort (there are 9 men in position to block along the line). The formation is named in the huddle as "Double Tight Slot." The alignment is illustrated in diagram 1-6.

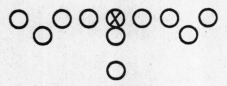

Diagram 1-6

In order to complete all the alignments by position, the offense deploys only a single set back. This single set back will be referred to as the fullback. He aligns his heels 13 feet from the ball, directly behind the quarterback. Because a great deal of the Double Slot offense is based on an initial ride fake to the fullback, this position best enables him to carry out his basic techniques. When running sprint out and roll out pass action, where the fullback must attack the defensive end, he lines up a bit deeper (16 feet) so that he can best clear the quarterback action and block the end defender. This slight depth adjustment poses no specific key for the defense; it is difficult at best to measure the depth of the fullback from their vantage points.

The quarterback takes a conventional "T" formation position.

MOTION TYPES

For the Double Slot to maximize its effectiveness in running and passing, it is essential to place one of the halfbacks in motion. This changes the formation and at the same time forces a change in alignment or a mental adjustment within the defense. Three types of motion will be used. Each is given a name and designated as follows: "motion," "jet," "fly." "Motion" and "jet" are used primarily in the passing attack. They are designed to force a defensive secondary adjustment. "Fly" is incorporated more with the running attack (also used in play action passes) and is designed to position one of the halfbacks in the backfield to become a more effective ball carrier.

Diagram 1-7 shows the "motion" call. This maneuver has the halfback moving quickly from one side of the formation to the other. The quarterback may call the snap count whenever he feels the motioning halfback has created a desirable adjustment in the defense. Generally the

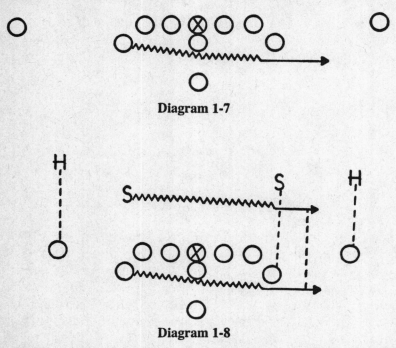

Diagram 1-7

Diagram 1-8

quarterback calls for the snap sometime after the motion man gets outside the other halfback's position. The defense reacts by going to a man-to-man coverage or shows a pre-rotation type zone once the motion man reaches a certain point. Diagrams 1-8 and 1-9 illustrate these situations. In 1-8 the safety man chases across the formation and plays man-to-man on the motioning halfback. In 1-9 the secondary pre-rotates on invert action once the motion man gets outside the stationary halfback. There are many coverage possibilities, but these offer two examples of how a particular secondary may react to motion. Few adjustments are made with the defensive linemen and linebackers when encountering a 4 deep secondary. Three deep defenses will "drop off" and adjust with an outside linebacker. Diagram 1-10 shows a 4-4 defense with an adjustment by the outside linebacker to motion.

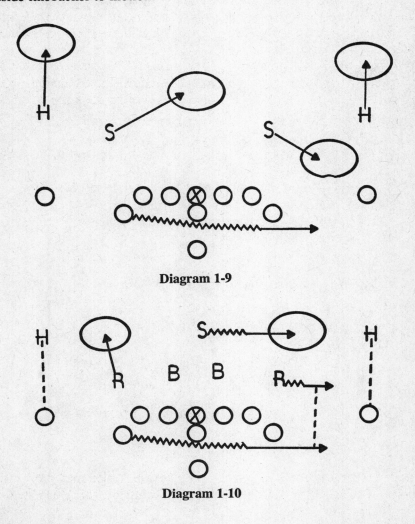

Diagram 1-9

Diagram 1-10

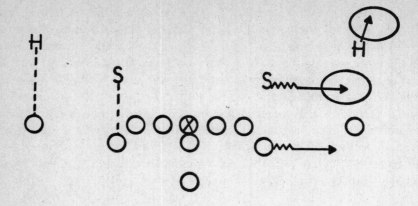

Diagram 1-11

Diagram 1-11 depicts "jet" motion. This technique places the halfback in motion to the outside of the formation in the direction of the split end. It establishes the popular "twins" formation. All the advantages inherent in the twin set can be utilized from this type of motion (primarily concerning passing strategies). "Jet" motion usually forces the defense to adjust with man-to-man coverage to the motion side. Three deep defenses will rotate the safety over or adjust the outside linebacker on the motion side. Diagram 1-12 shows a 3-deep adjustment to "jet" motion. The adjustment puts the outside linebacker in man-to-man coverage on the halfback; a desired mismatch should the halfback have superior speed and overall ability.

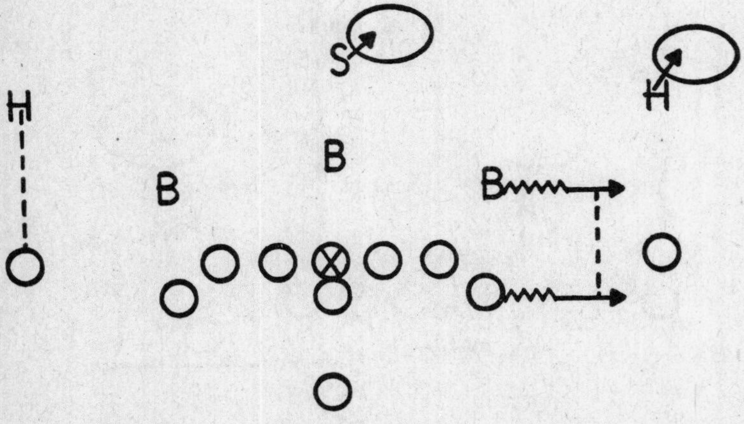

Diagram 1-12

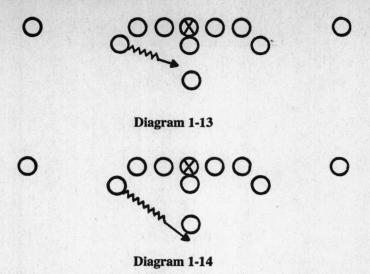

Diagram 1-13

Diagram 1-14

"Fly" motion is illustrated in diagram 1-13. This motion is most frequently used in the running game. The halfback may be placed in a number of positions, depending on the length and duration of the motion. He may end up in the position of a set halfback (behind the guard) or in the same alignment as a tailback in the "I" formation (directly in tandem behind the fullback). When running play action passes this motion gets a considerable amount of usage. Diagram 1-13 shows the "fly" motion establishing a halfback position, while diagram 1-14 shows the tailback alignment by the motion man. Most of the time "fly" motion will force an adjustment within the defensive forcing unit (linemen and linebackers). The offense must be prepared to run counter plays and related play action to offset these defensive adjustments.

HUDDLE

Diagram 1-15 shows the basic huddle alignment. This style is preferred in that it is easier to get the attention of the quarterback from the sidelines. The quarterback is in a better position so that all the offensive players can look at him, enhancing his poise and leadership role. The quarterback is in a good position to call plays and communicate directly with the offensive team.

In this huddle formation the back row consists of the offensive line.

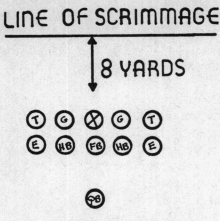

Diagram 1-15

They stand with their backs to the line of scrimmage. The front row is made up of the fullback in the middle, flanked by a halfback on each side. The two ends line up on each side of the halfback. The front row faces the quarterback and places their hands on their knees to allow the back row of linemen to view the quarterback. The huddle is formed 8 yards from the line of scrimmage. This allows the offense to position itself quickly so that more offensive plays can be run and time utilized as much as possible.

NAMING THE PLAY

Once the quarterback forms the huddle and is ready to call the next play, he gives the offense the following information:

1) Formation and motion type.
2) Play number and description.
3) Snap count.

This information is given twice. All players then clap their hands and yell, "Break!" moving quickly to the line of scrimmage. The split ends must move quickly into position and take a 3-point stance according to their hash mark rules. The interior linemen position themselves in a pre-stance (semi-crouched with elbows on knees) waiting for the quarterback to move under the center. The fullback and halfbacks also make their correct alignment and get right down into their stance. Halfbacks will use a 3-point stance with a maximum toe-instep foot position. The fullback may use a 3- or 4-point stance—one designed to give him the most efficient technique in moving laterally with equal effectiveness. Interior linemen can use a 3- or 4-point stance depending on the individual coach's preference. Offensive linemen are required to execute a great deal of mobility and the offensive stance should be one that facilitates this mobility.

As the quarterback sets under the center he places the interior linemen in their stance on the command "Set!" Next the quarterback calls a number to place one of the backs in the desired motion. He will call the snap count next and this may be delayed in order to allow the motion back to get into position and or to read an adjustment by the defense. The word "Go!" is used for the starting count and is yelled out by the quarterback in a non-rythmical tone of voice. For example the quarterback may want to have the ball snapped on 3; that means the 3rd "Go." He would come to the line and get the team set, have the halfback start in motion, and call out "Go!, (pause), Go!, Go!" The ball would be snapped on the third "Go." The non-rhythmical snap count takes extra practice and discipline, but can be used in situations to draw the defense offside, keeping them honest.

Plays incorporate both numbers and word descriptions. The word description names the particular play series while the number names the primary ball carrier and the hole number through which he must carry the ball. Example, "36 Belly" would break down as follows: "Belly" describes the play series; "3" names the fullback as the ball carrier and "6" describes the hole area over which he is to run.

All the backs are assigned numbers as illustrated in diagram 1-16. The fullback is assigned #3, the right halfback #4, the left halfback #1 and the quarterback #2.

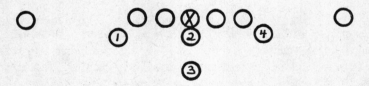

Diagram 1-16

Holes along the offensive line are presented in diagram 1-17. Each hole develops over a particular offensive linemen. The holes are numbered consecutively from left to right as illustrated. Each of these holes extends laterally to the position of the next offensive linemen inside and outside. Vertically the hole extends to the opponent's goal line. Diagram

Diagram 1-17

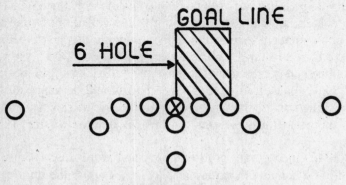

Diagram 1-18

1-18 shows the "6" hole represented by the shaded region. Laterally "6" extends to head on the center and head on the right offensive tackle. Generally the more efficiently blockers clear the hole laterally and seal it off from pursuit vertically will determine the degree of success for a given offensive play.

LINE BLOCKING RULES

Line play in the Double Slot offense is based on a numbering of defenders from the center out on each side. These defenders are numbered consecutively and each offensive linemen is assigned to block a particular numbered defender. In general terms the offensive center will block the #0 defender. The guard #1 and the tackle #2. If a tight end formation is used and depending on the play to be run, he will block #3. This system is kept as simple as possible with minimum adjustments. It allows the offensive linemen to really concentrate on execution and technique. Diagram 1-19 shows the 5-2 defense and how the numbering system is adapted to this alignment. Diagrams 1-20A-N illustrate a chart of the common defensive alignments and how they are numbered using the

Double Slot offense. Individual line techniques will be covered as the offense is developed in the following chapters.

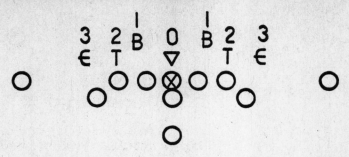

Diagram 1-19

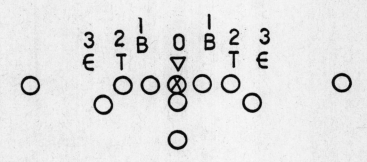

Diagram 1-20A

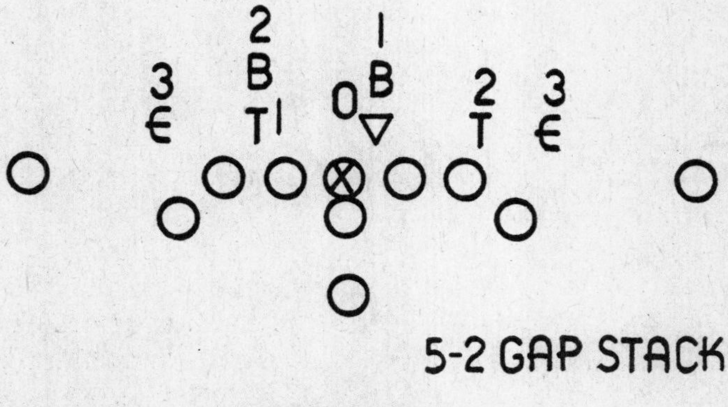

5-2 GAP STACK

Diagram 1-20B

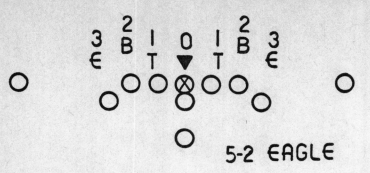

5-2 EAGLE

Diagram 1-20C

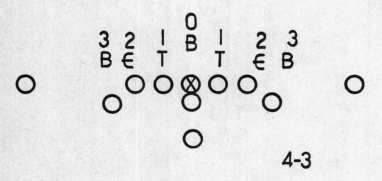

4-3

Diagram 1-20D

4-3 COLLEGE

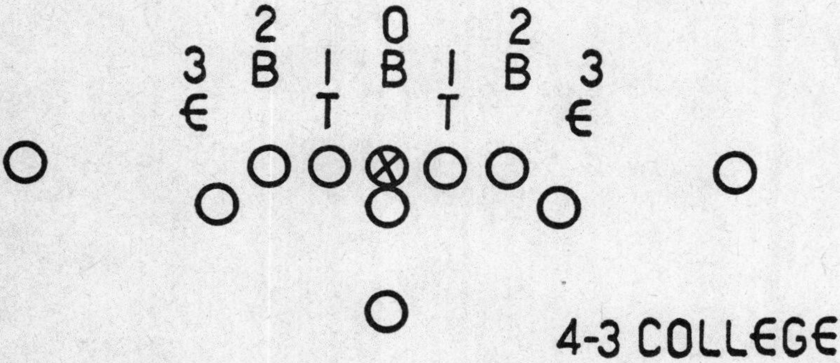

Diagram 1-20E

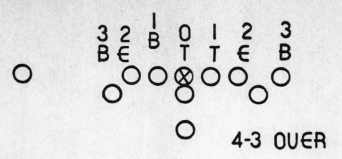

Diagram 1-20F

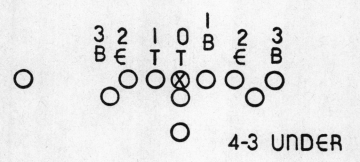

Diagram 1-20G

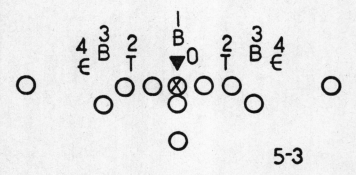

Diagram 1-20H

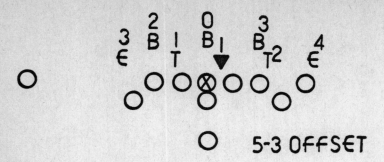

5-3 OFFSET

Diagram 1-20I

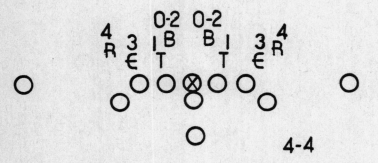

4-4

Diagram 1-20J

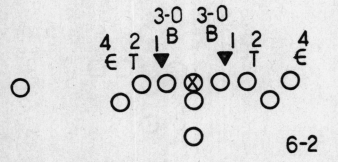

6-2

Diagram 1-20K

WIDE TACKLE 6

Diagram 1-20L

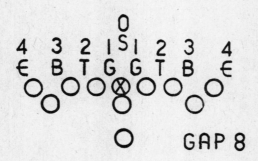

GAP 8

Diagram 1-20M

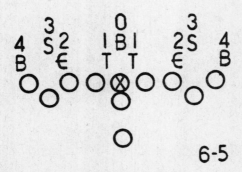

6-5

Diagram 1-20N

2

Coaching the Double Slot Veer Series

The Double Slot running attack centers around the Fullback Veer series. Establishing the fullback as the primary inside runner is essential for the evolution of other play patterns based on the Double Slot formation. Because the fullback is the only set back, he must be enough of an inside threat so that the defense must use at least two members of the forcing unit (linemen and linebackers) to monitor his movements. At the very minimum the defense should assign the fullback threat to one of its linebackers. Most of the time this linebacker will be playing the fullback from an inside-out angle, making a consistent number of tackles difficult.

FULLBACK VEER

To establish the fullback's inside threat and effect the most efficient ball exchange, the Veer course and quarterback hand-off from the Wishbone is best. The quarterback makes the hand-off behind the line of scrimmage, while the fullback has direction to cut inside or outside of the tackle's block. After the hand-off, the quarterback carries out a fake option. This fake is most important in that it sets the defense for the option plays in the Veer series. The option threat forces the defense to play a wide front, enhancing the inside running of the fullback. Also, with the release of potential receivers, the defense must respect the pass and defense the field in width and depth. Other plays in the series are derived from the basic fullback Veer action. This series features a strong inside running game by the fullback (Veer), Options (double and triple), and a Power Off-Tackle (Halfback Slant).

Diagrams 2-1A and 2-1B show the fullback Veer play against two basic defensive fronts (the 5-2 and 4-4). The play calling system desig-

33

nates this play as the 36 Veer (to the right) and 34 Veer (to the left). The fullback is the first number (he is the #3 back) and the hole he is to run by the second digit (each lineman is numbered). This play is directed at two members of the defense most likely assigned to monitor the fullback's movements. Important in the development of this entire series are the fakes of other dimensions of this play—namely the options and pass threats: these all aid in controlling defensive maneuvers.

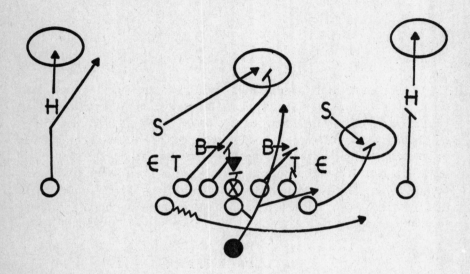

Diagram 2-1A

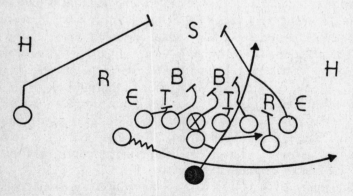

Diagram 2-1B

The assignments and techniques for the Fullback Veer play are as follows:

Playside end—If tight, block the inside linebacker then the near safety.

If split, slow block the deep outside 1/3.

Playside tackle—Drive block the second defender from the ball.

Playside guard—Drive block the first defender from the ball.

Center—Drive block #0.

Backside guard—Drive block the first defender from the ball.

Backside tackle—Drive block the second defender from the ball. Release inside #2 on the backside.

Backside end—If tight, block the middle 1/3.

If split, block the middle 1/3.

Playside halfback—Drive block #3; "arc" block pitch support.

Backside halfback—Drive for the sideline and fake a pitch reception. Work for the proper pitch relationship with the quarterback (4 yards deep in the backfield and 4 yards outside the quarterback).

Quarterback—Open pivot and mesh with the fullback. Hand-off the ball. Accelerate down the line and fake the option. Study the techniques of the perimeter defenders in their reactions to the option fake.

Fullback—Open with a six inch lead step, mesh with the quarterback and receive the hand-off. Slash at the "6" hole (guard-tackle gap). Cut inside or outside on the block of the playside tackle. Cross the line of scrimmage with the shoulders square to the goal line. Sprint, drive and break tackles.

BLOCKING CALLS

A variety of blocking schemes are incorporated to effectively establish the running game by the fullback. Different defensive alignments cause numerous problems for offensive blockers. Outlined below is a brief description of these alignments and blocking patterns used against them.

"Combo"—A combination block by the playside guard and tackle. Used against "gap stack" defensive alignments. It is a cooperation block where both offensive players work to-

gether to eliminate two defenders. The technique is outlined below.

Technique: The call is made by the offensive tackle. On
the snap the guard drive blocks through the outside hip of
the defender attempting to turn him to the inside. The
tackle drives to the inside blocking through the defender's outside armpit. This helps the guard gain leverage
on his block. The tackle now slides upfield and blocks the
linebacker. It is important that the tackle get his head between the linebacker and the ball carrier. Diagram 2-2
shows the "combo" call vs. the 4-4 defense.

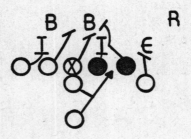

Diagram 2-2

"Step"—Another cooperation block between the guard and tackle.
This time the tackle drives inside taking the down defender, while the guard pulls around and blocks the
linebacker. It is important for the guard to keep his
shoulders parallel to the line of scrimmage. To accomplish this he must reach for the butt of the offensive
tackle with his outside hand and pull himself around. The
guard must move quickly to keep the correct geometric
relationship with the linebacker. When blocking the
linebacker it is equally important that the guard keep his
head between the defender and the ballcarrier. The
"step" technique is shown in diagram 2-3 against the 4-4
defense.

"A" Block—A call used by the center and backside guard to
counter common stunts between the middle guard and
linebackers in the 5-3 and 5-2 defenses.

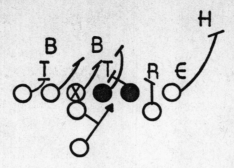

Diagram 2-3

Technique:

Center - Fire through the playside hip of the defensive **guard**. If the defender slants to the playside, stay with him on the block. Should the middle guard slant backside, come straight upfield and pick off the flowing linebacker.

Backside Guard—Aim for the playside hip of the middle guard (use a minimum split of 2 feet or less). As the middle guard slants to the backside, drive block him all the way. If the defender slants playside, turn upfield and block the near linebacker.

Diagram 2-4 shows "A" blocking against a 5-2 stunt.

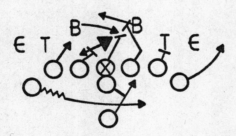

Diagram 2-4

Diagram 2-5 shows the 5-2 again but with a "stack" adjustment in an attempt to seal the primary running area of the fullback. A good "combo" block by the guard and tackle should make the basic Veer quite effective.

In diagram 2-6 a variation of the 4-4 is illustrated. This alignment takes the 2 inside linebackers and stacks them to give the offense an "odd" man defensive look.

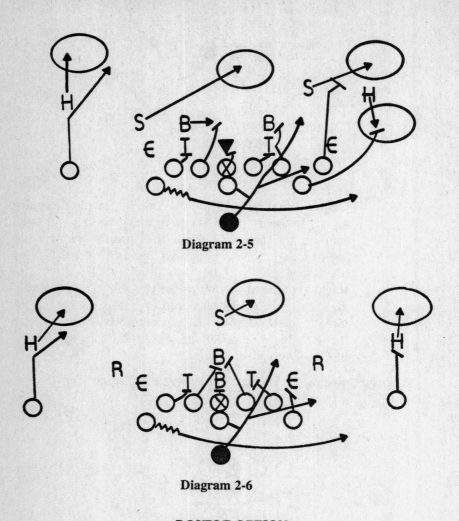

Diagram 2-5

Diagram 2-6

DOUBLE OPTION

Directly complementing the Fullback Veer play is the Double Option. This is a predetermined run or pitch by the quarterback. There is a strong inside fake of the Fullback Veer, and the quarterback keeps the ball optioning the defender on the end of the defensive alignment. The Double Option gets its name from the two dimensions that the quarterback executes (keep-pitch) as determined by the defensive end's reaction to the play. It is an extension of the Veer play and is actually being faked when the predetermined fullback play (Veer) is being run. Because the fullback does not receive the ball, he can act as a blocker, especially if the offense encounters trouble with inside stunts. The fullback must execute a good fake so that he gets tackled on the play. This will cancel the pursuit of one more defender and prevent him from escaping into the perimeter to disrupt the option. Diagram 2-7A and B illustrate the Double Option play against 2 basic defenses. Practically all the assignments are the same as for the Fullback Veer play. There is a slight change in technique at a few positions that will be so emphasized.

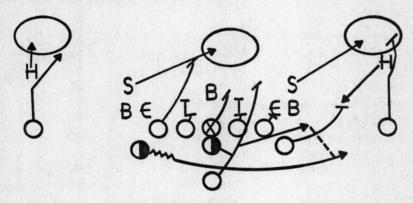

Diagram 2-7A

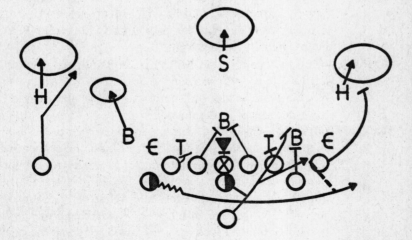

Diagram 2-7B

Assignments and techniques for the Double Option are outlined below.

Playside end—Release and block the deep outside 1/3. (*Note:* When the end releases he works for a position 1 yard in front of and 2 yards outside the defensive back. The end maintains this position until the defender recognizes that the play is a run and begins to react upfield. The end will stay on his feet and execute a pass blocking technique keeping himself between the defender and the ball carrier).

Playside linemen—Execute veer blocking. (*Note:* The playside tackle must work his head past the outside hip of the defender in the 5-2 defense.)

Center—Execute veer blocking.

Backside line—Execute veer blocking.

Backside end—Veer techniques.

Playside halfback—Check the position of #3. Execute "arc" block.

"Arc" technique: Drop step with the inside foot and work laterally to the outside. Block the defender responsible for supporting the pitch. Work to get the helmet past the defender's outside hip. Try to step on the defender's toes before blocking through his outside thigh. The "arc" technique is used against 4 deep defenses (7 man fronts), while the playside back will drive block #3 vs. 3 deep defenses (8 man fronts).

Fullback—Run the veer course. Make an excellent fake. Get tackled or block a linebacker. Concentrate on faking and blocking as the ball will be disconnected and carried by the quarterback to the outside.

Backside halfback—Go in "fly" motion as in the veer play. On the snap, drive for the sidelines and establish the proper pitch relationship with the quarterback. Be ready for an early pitch as the quarterback may be forced to dump the ball quickly as a result of immediate defensive pressure. Be sure to look the ball in when the quarterback makes the pitch. Cut on the blocks of the playside end and halfback.

Quarterback—Fake the veer play to the fullback. *Accelerate* down the line at the end defender. Should the defender stay planted or move upfield to tackle the pitchman, tuck the ball away and turn up into the defense. If the defensive end crashes on the quarterback, deliver the ball to the halfback right now.

SPECIAL TECHNIQUES FOR THE QUARTERBACK

1) *Making the pitch.* The pitch is made with one arm. The outside arm is extended with a loose wrist action. This will insure that the ball is floating to the pitch man. The pass should be firm with a flat trajectory.

2) *Reading a "feathering" defender.* This technique is used against a defensive end that strings the play out and attempts both to play the quarterback and to be in good position to tackle the pitchman should the toss be made. The defender attempts to disrupt the pitch relationship between the halfback and the quarterback. It makes the quarterback pitch the ball deep in the backfield (at a greater than 45 degree angle) to the halfback. To counter this technique the quarterback must accelerate to the outside shoulder of the "feathering" defender and pitch the ball. The quarterback must make the defender play him or commit to the pitch coverage.

3) *Collision at the meshpoint.* On occasion the defense will get penetration and tackle the fullback during the ride fake or at the exact instant of the disconnect. This is especially true when running the option to the split end side. The quarterback must be ready for a flash ride fake to the fullback. It is a good idea to locate the end defender as quickly as possible when running at the split end side. Should a collision at the mesh point take place, the quarterback must step around the collision and work back towards the line of scrimmage as he delivers the pitch. If the end defender tackles the fullback, the quarterback options the next defender to show. Most likely this will be a linebacker so it is a good idea to have the quarterback deliver the pitch as soon as he gets around the collision point.

SPECIAL BLOCKING CALLS AND ADJUSTMENTS

All of the blocking schemes for the Fullback Veer play can be utilized in the Double Option. These include the "combo," "step" and "A" blocking schemes. Because the option play is directed to the defensive perimeter, the offense will encounter a varying degree of perimeter tactics by the defense. As a change up the offense can use two blocking variations by the playside halfback and split end. Frequently when running the option to the split end side a great deal of "invert" action by one of the inside safeties is encountered. The "X" blocking scheme is used as an effective change up against invert action.

"*X*" *call*– This blocking scheme has the split end driving inside and blocking the forcing inside safety. The playside halfback will use the "arc" course and block the deep outside 1/3. The "X" call is used because of the difficulty that the playside halfback may have in blocking the inverting defender. It is easy for the defender to slip in behind the "arc" blocker and tackle the pitch man. Diagram 2-8 shows the "X" call vs. the invert rotation.

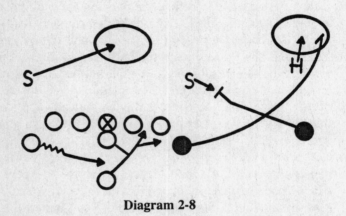

Diagram 2-8

Techniques on the "X" call

Split end—Split out a maximum of 12 yards. Actually 10 yards is a better working distance. Release flat down the line and work upfield for a depth of 4 to 6 yards. Block the safety *above the waist*. Get the helmet in front and swing the hips upfield. This will seal both escape routes for the defender.

Playside halfback—Execute the "arc" technique. Work for a position 2 yards outside and 1 yard in front of the deep 1/3 defender. Maintain this position until the defender reacts to the run, then execute a pass block on him staying between the defender and the ball carrier.

The "X" call is used against 3 and 4 deep defenses that feature invert rotation to the split end side.

The second blocking call is used primarily against 4 deep defenses that "feather" the defensive end to cover the pitchman and at the same time attack the quarterback with one of the inside safeties. As the quarterback works down the line and sees the end's move to the outside he reacts by keeping the ball and turning directly upfield. What the quarterback does not see is the safetyman coming straight up and tackling him on the line of scrimmage. The blocking adjustment assigns the playside halfback to release straight upfield and attack the safetyman on a flat angle. Even if the safety uses invert action towards the outside, the offensive halfback is still in good position to block the defender by attacking him on a flatter angle. This blocking call is referred to as the "lead" technique. (The playside halfback "leads" straight upfield). Diagram 2-9 shows this "lead" technique by the playside halfback.

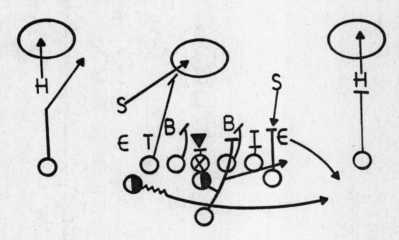

Diagram 2-9

TRIPLE OPTION

The triple option extends the optioning concept to one more dimension. This extra dimension will be referred to as the hand-off key—the first defender on or outside the playside offensive tackle. A reaction by that defender will determine a hand-off to the fullback or a disconnect and option by the quarterback. All the "reads" fall on the shoulders of the quarterback. Generally if the hand-off key stays in place or charges straight upfield, the quarterback will give the ball to the fullback. Should the "key" slant inside to tackle the fullback, then the quarterback will remove the ball from the ride action and execute the double option to the outside. Interior blocking assignments are now varied so that an inside crease for the fullback is created. The crease is nothing more than a running lane for the fullback with all defenders inside this crease walled off from pursuit and all defenders outside the crease left unblocked so that they can be read and eliminated by the quarterback's reactions.

Diagrams 2-10 A and B show the triple being run against two standard defensive alignments.

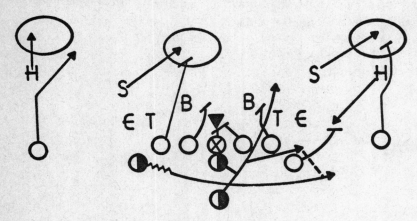

Diagram 2-10A

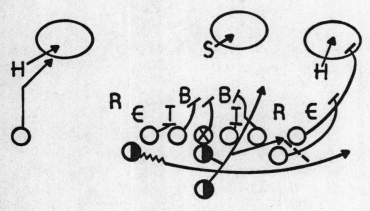

Diagram 2-10B

The following is an outline of individual assignments and techniques for the Triple Option.

Playside end—Block double option.

Playside tackle—Drive block the first defender inside, on, or off the line of scrimmage.

Playside guard—Block the first defender on the line of scrimmage. Double team with the center on a middle guard in the 5-2 defense. Block the middle linebacker in the 5-3 defense.

Center—Block #0.

Backside linemen—Execute veer blocking assignments.

Backside end—Release shallow and block the middle 1/3.

Playside halfback—"arc" block the pitch support.

Backside halfback—Establish the proper pitch relationship with the quarterback.

Fullback—Execute the veer play. Be ready to receive the ball from the quarterback. Make the cut on the block of the playside tackle. Should the quarterback disconnect, block the first linebacker on his pursuit course.

Quarterback—Carry out the triple option techniques. Read the first defender on or outside the playside tackle. Locate the defender before the snap.

1) Should the defender move straight across the line of scrimmage or stay in position, give the ball to the fullback.

2) If the defender slants hard inside, disconnect the ball and execute the double option on the defensive end.

Special techniques for the quarterback

Often when running the triple option to the split end side the defense will attack the mesh point of the fullback and quarterback. Both the quarterback and fullback get tackled and the play is effectively stopped before getting too far underway. In some situations it is advantageous for the quarterback to take the snap and not even ride the fullback, but keep the ball on his stomach and at the most jab the ball at the fullback. As the quarterback opens, he immediately places the ball on his stomach, while locating the hand-off key. If the give looks good, he jabs the ball into the fullback's pocket. If, because of defensive penetration, the give looks bad he is in a better position to carry out the double option dimension of the play. If the hand-off key and the end defender both slant hard to the inside, the quarterback is in a much better position to deliver the pitch quickly. The offense should keep this technique in mind especially when running the "triple" to the split end side. Because the two outside defenders are left unblocked and the distance to the mesh point is so short, this defensive tactic is seen quite frequently.

BLOCKING ADJUSTMENTS AND VARIATIONS

1) The split end and playside halfback may use "X" and "lead" blocking variations as outlined under the double option.

2) The interior line utilizes a couple of variations that aid in the isolation of the hand-off key. Both of these are primarily applicable to the 5-2 defense. For other defenses the "combo" and "step" techniques can be utilized. The two 5-2 variations are as follows:

"Loop"—This blocking scheme helps to neutralize the common pinch-scrape stunt from the 5-2. The playside guard will fire out straight down the line and block the defensive tackle slanting inside. Should the tackle not slant down, the guard will turn upfield and block the inside linebacker. The playside tackle will fire out through the outside hip of the defensive tackle and block the flowing linebacker. (Note: If the defensive tackle steps to the outside with the offensive tackle, it is an automatic give by the quarterback. If the defender's helmet moves inside down the line it is an automatic option for the quarterback). If the defensive tackle does not slant, then the offensive tackle will block him and the option dimension of the play will develop. Diagrams 2-11 and 2-12 illustrate "loop" blocking vs. a slanting 5-2 defense. In 2-11 the defensive tackle slants to the inside and is blocked by the guard. In diagram 2-12 the offensive tackle and defensive tackle collide and the option phase of the triple develops.

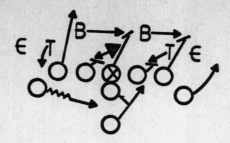

Diagram 2-11

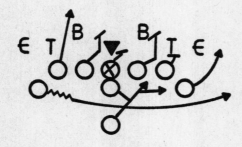

Diagram 2-12

3

Coaching Double Slot Complementary Veer Plays

The running plays in this chapter are further extensions of the basic Fullback Veer action. When the ball is snapped, the initial actions of the offense must match, in as many ways as possible, the basic movements of the Fullback Veer and Option plays. The initial actions must threaten the defense in width and depth, supporting the basic concept of the Double Slot offense.

Plays include a Power-Off Tackle, named the "Slant." The Slant is then extended into a "read" play where the quarterback will determine the hand-off to the fullback or slanting halfback running the ball off-tackle. The hand-off key for the play is the same as for the Triple Option (first defender on or outside the offensive tackle) and is isolated using triple option blocking schemes.

A further extension of the Fullback Veer and Slant plays features an option to the tight end coming back around as a pitchman after the fake of the Veer and Slant actions. The play is run from a double tight end formation. It is directed at defenses that have their perimeter men reacting from outside-in to give support on stopping the halfback on the Slant play. The tight end becomes the pitch man in an option play and receives the ball from the quarterback after a complete fake of the Slant action.

HALFBACK SLANT

The Halfback Slant play directs the motioning halfback off-tackle after the quarterback fakes the fullback on the Veer action. Diagram 3-1 shows the Slant play being run to the split end side of the formation with the playside halfback making the key block. Against the 5-2, as illustrated, the halfback must block the defensive tackle.

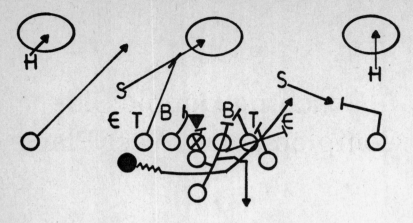

Diagram 3-1

At the snap the quarterback executes a veer fake to the fullback. The backside halfback goes in motion as he does on the option play. The ball carrier then drives hard through the fullback's original position, making it look as if he were running his option course. The halfback does not continue wide but cuts up inside and receives a hand-off from the quarterback. All linemen will block rule and the tight end turns out the defensive end. The playside halfback blocks #3 if the defense is an 8-man front or releases on his "lead" course if facing a 4-deep (7-man front). Diagrams 3-2A and B show the Slant play being run against two defensive fronts.

ASSIGNMENTS AND TECHNIQUES
FOR THE SLANT PLAY

Playside end—Align in a tight position. Drive the end defender to the outside. If split, release outside at the halfback; plant the outside foot and drive inside blocking the safety.

Playside linemen—Block veer rules. Use "combo" and "step" calls.

Center—Block #0. Use "A" call vs. stunting 5-2.

Backside linemen—Block veer rule.

Backside guard—Use "A" call against a stunting 5-2 defense.

Backside end—Release and block the middle 1/3.

Playside halfback— Check the position of #3. Block #3 if against an 8 man front. If faced with a 4 deep, release straight across the line and block the inside safety man. (Lead blocking call.)

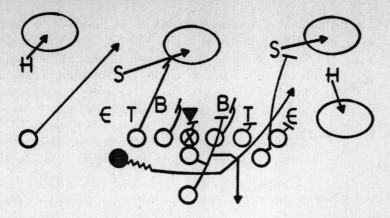

Diagram 3-2A

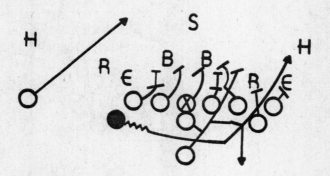

Diagram 3-2B

Fullback—Run the veer play and make an excellent fake. Block one of the linebackers after the fake into the line.

Backside halfback—Go in motion as in the fullback Veer play. On the snap drive hard through the original position of the fullback. The defense must think that the option play is developing. As the fullback is cleared, the halfback cuts upfield as close as possible to the fullback. Receive the ball from the quarterback and drive across the line of scrimmage as fast as possible. When crossing the line of scrimmage keep the shoulders parallel to the goal line. This will allow the breaking of arm tackles. The ball carrier must key the blocks of the tackle, the split end, and the playside halfback.

Quarterback—Execute the veer ride to the fullback. (*Technique:* Open at a 45-degree angle to the line of scrimmage. Place the ball in the fullback's pocket. Ride the fullback into the line). Disconnect the ball from the fullback and take a short lead step with the right foot (play being run to the right side); the football should be on the quarterback's stomach. As the halfback slants, place the ball in his pocket. After making the hand-off, drive down the line for two steps and then drop back to pass.

An alternate blocking scheme for the Slant is to utilize a pulling guard and apply the short trap technique. Diagrams 3-3 and 3-4 show the Slant play with the guard pulling against the 4-4 and 5-2 defenses. In run-

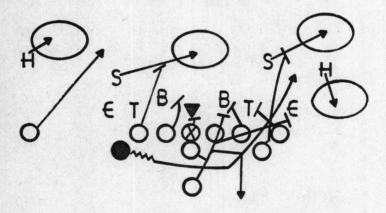

Diagram 3-3

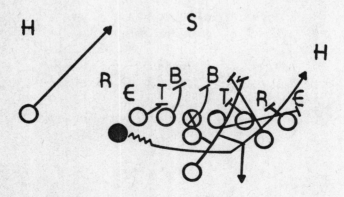

Diagram 3-4

ning the play against the 4-4 defense the "step" blocking call used in the veer is almost a pull by the guard, so even using this alternate blocking pattern, the defense initially receives a veer key. The assignments and techniques for the line are as follows. This blocking scheme is referred to as "G."

"G" BLOCKING ASSIGNMENTS
AND TECHNIQUES

Playside end—Align in a tight position. Drive inside on the first defender. It will be the outside linebacker in a 4-4 defense. Against the 5-2 drive block the defensive tackle. A "combo" block with the playside tackle may be used also against the 5-2 defense. The technique on the "combo" call is to drive inside through the near hip of the defensive tackle. This helps the tackle stabilize his block. Slide off the defensive tackle and drive upfield blocking the pursuing linebacker.

Playside tackle— Block the triple option assignment. If a "combo" call is made when facing the 5-2 defense, drive block the defensive tackle. Work the helmet past the outside hip of the defender. The tight end will drive down, slam the defensive tackle and slide upfield, blocking the linebacker. Should the defensive tackle slant to the inside, lock on and block him all the way down the line.

Playside guard—Pull and block the first defender that appears outside the block of the tight end. As the pull is made the guard must work up into the line. He must attack the de-

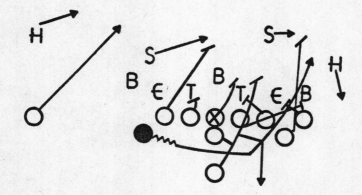

Diagram 3-5

fender from an inside-out position. As contact is made the blocker must hit with the same foot and same shoulder. The blocker must effectively take away the inside leg of the defender.

Center—Block Veer rule.

Backside linemen—Block Veer rules.

Backside end—Veer assignment.

Diagram 3-5 shows the Slant play against the 4-3 defense using "G" blocking. The fullback must "fill block" for the pulling guard. This means that he must help the playside tackle with his block on the defensive tackle. The fullback must concentrate on making an excellent hand-off fake and then aim for and explode through the outside thigh of the defensive tackle.

Diagrams 3-7 and 3-8 show the Slant play run to the split end side. In 3-7 the defense is a 4-4. The blocking is veer with a "step" block by the playside guard and tackle. Diagram 3-8 shows "G" blocking with a playside "combo" block by the halfback and tackle against a 5-2 defense.

SUMMARY OF BLOCKING CALLS AND
TECHNIQUES FOR THE SLANT

1) When rule blocking is used the linemen may use a "combo," "step" or "loop" call. Diagram 3-6 shows "loop" blocking against a slanting 5-2. The center and backside guard use "A" blocking.

2) "G" blocking. The tight end and tackle can execute a "combo" block between them. The center and backside guard may use an "A" call. A good fake and fill block by the fullback is essential. The fullback may fill on a linebacker (5-2 defense) or a down lineman.

RUNNING THE SLANT PLAY
WITH TRIPLE BLOCKING

The Triple Option blocking pattern can be used when running the Slant play. An optional hand-off can be carried out by the quarterback. This hand-off option is determined the same way as that of the Triple Option play. The quarterback will read the first defender on or outside the playside offensive tackle. If the defender charges upfield or stays in position, the quarterback will give the ball to the fullback. Should the "read" defender charge inside and play the fullback, then the quarterback will hand the ball to the backside halfback on the Slant play. The only excep-

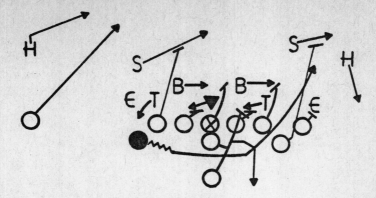

Diagram 3-6

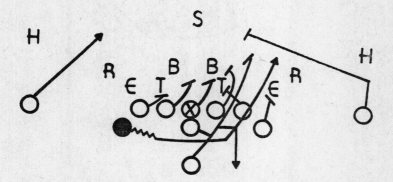

Diagram 3-7

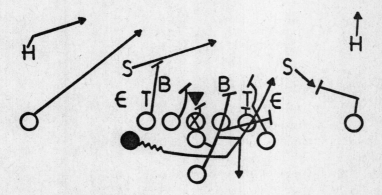

Diagram 3-8

tion in the triple blocking is that of the playside end and halfback. The tight end formation is used to run this play. The halfback executes a screen block on the hand-off key, while the tight end must block the defensive end to the outside. Both of these blocks establish an outside running crease for the backside halfback. Diagrams 3-9A and B illustrate the "slant read" play.

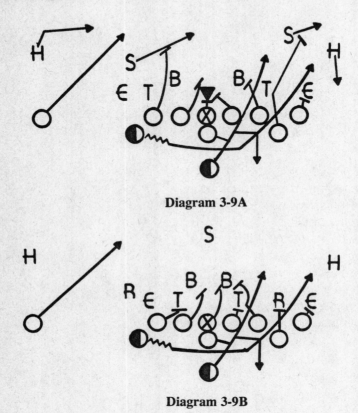

Diagram 3-9A

Diagram 3-9B

TECHNIQUES FOR THE "SLANT READ" PLAY

Playside end—Line up as a tight end. Drive block the first defender to the outside.

Playside linemen—Block the triple option.

Center—Block the triple option.

Backside linemen—Block the veer play.

Backside end—Triple option assignment.

Playside halfback—Drive through the outside hip of the hand-off key. (*Note:* The hand-off key is the first defender on or outside the tackle). By blocking through the outside hip, the defender is influenced to react to the outside against pressure.

Fullback—Execute the Veer. Should the ball be disconnected, explode into one of the pursuing inside linebackers.

Quarterback—Open pivot and execute the mesh with the fullback. Locate the hand-off key and give the ball to the fullback if the defender is stationary or moves directly upfield. Should the defender move inside down the line, pull the ball out of the fullback's pocket and hand-off to the backside halfback.

Backside halfback—Run the slant play. If the ball is handed off explode across the line of scrimmage on the blocks of the playside end and halfback. Be sure to make an excellent fake if the ball is not handed off.

The purpose of the block by the playside halfback is two fold: First, when blocking the hand-off key the defender may think the ball is going outside of him because of the blocking position of the halfback (driving the defender to the inside). A false pressure reaction is set up in the mind of the hand-off key, and if he fights pressure to the outside, the fullback dimension of the play should go. Second, should the hand-off key react to the inside release of the offensive tackle and close down to shut off the fullback, then the block by the halfback is a great deal easier. The halfback contains the hand-off key and screens the defender off from the outside running lane.

END OPTION

As defenses become more and more exposed to the Slant play and Slant read, they develop certain keys and reactions to the various dimensions of these plays. Techniques are developed that aid in pursuit and allow the defense to outnumber the offense at the point of attack. The most common adjustment takes place in the defensive secondary. Both the defensive halfback and safety will key the blocks of the tight end and playside halfback. Should both the halfback and end block, then the safety and defensive halfback will support on pursuit inside the block of the tight end. Diagram 3-10 shows the angles of pursuit taken by the safety and halfback to outnumber the play at the point of attack. The filling corner and safety can effectively seal the running lanes. Diagram 3-11 shows a 3-deep secondary reacting with similar moves. The safety and halfback both support to the inside against the Slant play.

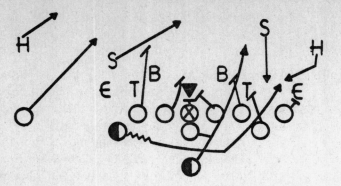

Diagram 3-10

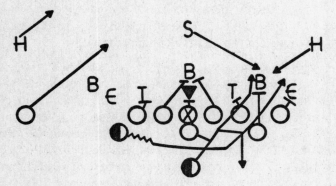

Diagram 3-11

The offense can run the Slant play and force this defensive reaction. This defensive maneuver can be controlled by faking both hand-offs and pitching the ball to a trailing tight end. To best experience this play a two tight end formation is used. Actually the quarterback options the first defender that shows outside the playside tight end's block. Diagram 3-12 shows the End Option against the 4-4 defense.

TECHNIQUES FOR THE END OPTION

Playside end—Line up in a tight position. Drive block the defensive end. This block will cause the defensive end to react back to the inside (false pressure). A steady exposure to the slant play should make the defensive end inside conscious in an effort to close the halfback's running lane.

Playside linemen—Block the triple option.

Center—Block the triple option.

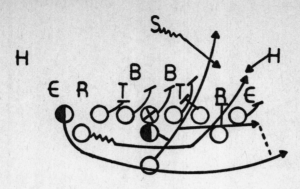

Diagram 3-12

Backside linemen—Block triple.

Backside end—Step back to the inside with the inside foot. Come away from the line of scrimmage at a 20 degree angle. Drive for a position 1 yard deeper than the fullback's original position. Sprint wide and work for a position 4 yards deep and 4 yards wider than the quarterback. Look for the pitch as the quarterback gets around the block of the playside tight end.

Playside halfback—Drive Block #3 if an 8 man front. "Lead" on the safety if a 7-man front (4 deep).

Fullback—Run the veer play. When the quarterback disconnects the ball, block one of the linebackers.

Backside halfback—Go in motion and fake the Slant play. Make a good fake to get tackled on the play.

Quarterback—Fake the Slant play. Disconnect the ball from the backside halfback and get around the block of the tight end. Option the first defender to show. Keep the ball if the defender moves to cover the end. Pitch the ball if the defender commits to the quarterback.

4

Coaching the Double Slot Buck Series

The plays in this chapter are based on a series of play actions made popular by the Wing T offense. One of the most common play patterns run by Wing T teams is the Buck series. In these plays three dimensions of the defense are threatened. First, the fake of the fullback up the middle aids as a check on interior pursuit by linebackers. The backside halfback attacking the defensive corner is the second dimension. The third is the quarterback carrying out bootleg action after one of the hand-offs (either the fullback or halfback). All the plays incorporate these three basic movements. A complete series of pass plays can be developed from this play action. In diagram 4-1 a Wing T formation is shown running the Buck Sweep play to the strong side (towards the wingback). The same play when run from the Double Slot formation will closely resemble the Wing T sweep depicted in 4-1.

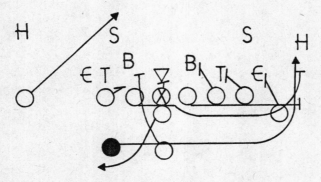

Diagram 4-1

FULLBACK BUCK DIVE

The Buck Dive action directs the fullback on a quick thrust up the middle of the defense. Two blocking schemes will be incorporated. One involves basic rule blocking, while the other features a short trap scheme. Diagram 4-2 shows the Dive play run at the 5-2 defense. Because of the path run by the fullback, this is one of the quickest hitting plays in football. It is important that other members of the offense carry out their fakes not only to enhance the effectiveness of the fullback but also to aid in the subsequent development of plays in this series. The primary faking areas involve the backside halfback carrying out the sweep and the quarterback faking the bootleg action to the backside. Thus as the play action threatens both flanks, the middle of the defense is quickly attacked.

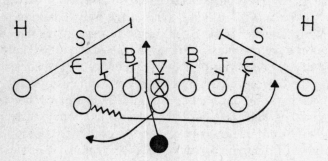

Diagram 4-2

ASSIGNMENTS FOR THE BUCK DIVE

Playside end—If split, release outside at the defensive halfback for 3 steps. Plant the outside foot and drive inside for the safetyman.
If tight, release shallow and concentrate on blocking the middle safety.

Playside tackle—Drive block #2. Against the 4-4 defense block the playside defensive tackle. This assignment is shown in diagram 4-3.

Playside guard—Drive block #1. Against the 4-4 block the playside defensive tackle.

Center—Drive block #0. Against the 4-4, block the playside inside linebacker. If the linebacker scrapes to the outside, wall him off from the inside. Otherwise drive him to the outside. The fullback will be running straight up the middle. When blocking a middle guard, the center must use the following technique as the fullback is cutting on the center's block.

Special technique—In running at the 5-2 or 5-3 defense, the block of the center is the most critical and will directly affect the outcome of the play. The center takes a short step with his playside foot at the middle guard. He must block higher than usual and under control. If the middle guard slants away from the play, the center should be in a balanced position and adjust with the defender. If the defender plays a reading technique, the center must turn his butt to the hole and wall off the middle guard. The key is for the center to come off the ball higher and under control; this will prevent the center over-stepping and losing balance. The fullback will cut opposite the middle guard's move. This play allows the guards to get good blocks on the linebackers (5-2 defense). This technique also cuts down on the slant tactics of the middle guard. It forces the defender to play more of a reading technique.

Backside guard—Drive block #1. Against the 4-4, slam the defensive tackle and explode upfield on the backside inside linebacker. This technique is illustrated in diagram 4-4.

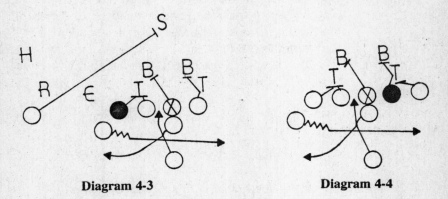

Diagram 4-3   Diagram 4-4

Backside tackle—Drive block #2. Against the 4-4 drive inside on the defensive tackle and stop his penetration. The guard will slam him and release upfield on the linebacker. This might be thought of as an inside "combo" block. Be careful not to drive the defender too far inside. Attempt to make him react to pressure from the outside. Try and cut him down if he attempts to charge inside. The slam technique of the guard should set up the defender.

Backside end—If split, release shallow across field and block the middle 1/3.

If tight, release downfield and block the middle 1/3.

Playside halfback—Drive block #3.

Backside halfback—Go in "fly" motion. Fake a handoff from the quarterback and drive hard, faking a sweep to the backside.

Fullback—If running this play to the left, aim for the left hip of the quarterback. Receive the hand-off and cut on the block of the center. Against the 5-2 defense cut opposite the move of the middle guard. Against the 4-4 watch the block of the center and backside guard; try to run the ball straight up the middle at the first crack of "daylight."

If running the play to the right, aim for the right hip of the quarterback and execute the same techniques.

Quarterback—When running the play to the left, open straight back with the left foot. Step back also with the right foot (don't congest the running lane of the fullback). The hand-off should be made as tight as possible to the fullback. After the hand-off drive back behind the playside guard and fake another hand-off to the motion halfback. Continue in this direction on a bootleg fake. As the bootleg is faked, check the reactions of the corner defenders. Determine the potential vulnerability of the defense to a bootleg keep.

**KEY COACHING POINTS
FOR THE BUCK DIVE PLAY**

1) The fakes must threaten both flanks as the fullback hits up the middle.
2) The center must block higher with a balanced stance.
3) The center must wall-off a slanting middle guard.
4) The fullback explodes at the correct hip of the quarterback.
5) The fullback cuts on the move of the middle guard. He also cuts on the blocks of the backside guard and center against the 4-4 defense.

6) The halfback goes in motion and fakes a sweep opposite the direction of the called Dive play.

7) The quarterback steps back straight with his foot on the side to which the play is run. The fullback should hit as straight ahead as possible, looking for the block on the middle guard.

8) A strong bootleg fake by the quarterback.

9) This play is directed over the "5" hole. That is over the offensive center. Because the center is assigned only a single number, the play is named as "35 Buck Dive." With a single number the offense must specify a direction as to which hip of the quarterback the fullback will aim. The words right or left are added at the end of the play call. Example: to run the play to the left, the huddle call would be made as "35 Buck Dive left."

FULLBACK BUCK TRAP

No fullback-oriented running attack is complete without a middle trap. Using buck action in the backfield results in the most effective and quickest hitting trap in football. The quarterback and backside halfback will continue with the same fakes as with the Buck Dive play. Again movements by other members of the offensive unit are important in setting up other running plays off this action. The Fullback Buck Trap is illustrated in diagram 4-5 against the 4-4 defense.

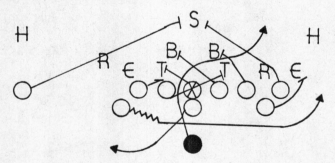

Diagram 4-5

TRAPPING ASSIGNMENTS AND TECHNIQUES

Playside end—If split, release and block the middle 1/3. A good block on the middle safety will result in a touchdown for the fullback. If tight, release shallow and block the middle 1/3.

Playside tackle—Drive block the first linebacker inside.

Playside guard—Drive block to the inside. If there is no defender inside on the line of scrimmage, pull and influence to the outside.

Situations for the playside guard:

1) Against the 5-2 defense, double team or "combo" block with the center.

2) Block the backside linebacker in the 4-4 defense. The 4-4 outnumbers the offense over the guards and center positions.

3) In the 5-3 defense, double team block with the center.

4) Against the 4-3 (6-1) the playside guard will influence to the outside. That is, block the first defender on the line of scrimmage to the outside. *Influence technique:* The first step is taken directly down the line as if executing a pulling technique. The second step is taken up into the line. Block the first defender that is encountered. Position the helmet so that it is on the side of the hole. The influence technique is designed to pull the defensive tackle to the outside, increasing the width of the hole. This is based on the concept that a defensive tackle is coached to get in the "hip pocket" of the offensive guard should he pull to the outside.

5) Another situation for the playside guard against the 4-3 (6-1) defense is when the middle linebacker fills immediately upon seeing the center block to the backside. The playside tackle cannot get a good block on the backer as he fills into the line of scrimmage. Because the playside guard is using an influence technique, the middle linebacker is free to make the tackle on the fullback. This situation is shown in diagram 4-6. Should the linebacker be reacting this way, the playside guard will not use the influence technique but drive block to the inside on the middle linebacker. Diagram 4-7 shows the guard blocking the middle linebacker as he fills because of the center's backside block.

Center—Drive block to the backside. If no backside block, drive the middle guard #0. The center must first check the backside and he will block in this direction against de-

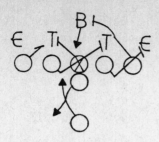
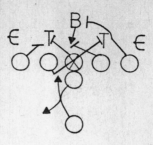

Diagram 4-6   Diagram 4-7

fenses that play linemen over the offensive guards (even
defensive alignments). He will double team with the
playside guard against a middle guard (odd defensive
alignments).

Backside guard—Pull and trap the first defender past the center.
The guard must take a short first step at the center. This
should take about a 1/4 turn in his body. On the second
step the guard must work into the line of scrimmage. As
contact is made the guard should be planting the same
foot as the shoulder with which he is to make contact. If
pulling to the right he will block with his right shoulder
and be planting his right foot as contact is made. He
should hit the defender at hip level and work up as
quickly as possible.

Backside tackle—Step down to the inside and fill the area vacated
by the pulling guard.

Backside end—If split, release and block the middle 1/3.
If tight, release and block the middle 1/3.

Backside halfback—Go in "fly" motion. Drive hard and fake the
sweep play.

Fullback—Execute the Buck Dive play. Follow the block of the
pulling backside guard. Against the 5-2 and 5-3 defenses
the hole will be more towards one side of the line. Generally this will be over the location of the playside guard.
Be ready to hit wider when running against "odd" defenses. The play will hit straight ahead against 4-3 and
4-4 defenses.

Quarterback—Run the Buck Dive technique. Clear the line so the
trapping guard will have room to pull. Carry out the
sweep and bootleg fakes.

Diagram 4-8 shows the Buck Trap against the 5-3 defense. Like the 5-2, the fullback must hit wider than directly over the center.

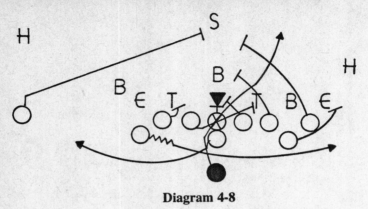

Diagram 4-8

NAMING THE BUCK TRAP

The call in the huddle for the fullback trap play would be made as follows: to the left, "36 Fullback Buck Trap"; to the right, "34 Fullback Buck Trap." The playside guard is used as a reference point for the running hole.

BUCK OFF-TACKLE

When the Buck Dive and Buck Sweep are being run emphasis is placed on having other members of the offense carry out fakes not only to develop the fullback Buck plays but also to threaten both defensive flanks. Specifically these fakes were by the quarterback, on a bootleg to one flank and a sweep fake by the backside halfback to the opposite flank.

The Buck Off-Tackle play directs the motioning halfback to the off-tackle hole with a great deal of sweep action. The effective fakes of the fullback and quarterback are essential in aiding the effectiveness of the Off-Tackle play. The fullback must fake the Buck Dive so that the inside out pursuit of the linebackers will be delayed. The quarterback must fake the bootleg so that the other defensive flank is threatened. The Buck Off-Tackle is illustrated in diagram 4-9 against the 5-2 defense.

ASSIGNMENTS FOR THE OFF-TACKLE PLAY

Playside end—If split, drive inside on the safety. If tight, drive block the first defender to the inside. Be ready for a

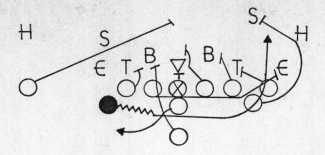

Diagram 4-9

"combo" call from the offensive tackle against a stunting 5-2 defense. See diagram 4-10 for the "combo" block.

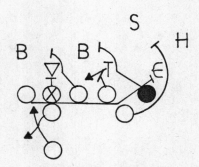

Diagram 4-10

Playside tackle—Drive block the first defender to the inside on or off the line of scrimmage. Against the 4-4 defense be ready for a "combo" or "step" call from the playside guard. Make a "combo" call with the tight end against the 5-2 stunts.

Playside guard—Drive block the man on. If no man on drive block the first defender to the inside. Use the "combo" and "step" calls against the 4-4. Double team with the center against the 5-2 and be ready to slide off the double team to cut off the flow of the backside linebacker. Block the middle linebacker in the 5-3 defense. Drive block the defensive tackle in the 4-3. When blocking the 4-3 (6-1) the middle linebacker may step and fill across the line when he sees the center block to the backside; should this happen then block inside and the tackle will take the defensive tackle alone.

Center—Drive block the first defender backside. If no defender on the backside, block the defender head on (5-2 and 5-3), the middle guard.

Backside guard—Pull and trap the first defender outside the block of the tight end. If running to the split end side then trap the first defender outside the playside halfback's block.

Backside tackle—Step to the inside and help the center with the backside block. The assignment is to fill the area vacated by the pulling guard.

Backside end—If split, release shallow and work across field. Block the middle 1/3. If tight, release shallow and work across the field. Get ahead of the play by staying shallow on the release course.

Playside halfback—If aligned to the tight end side, release tight to the end through the outside leg of the defensive end. The defender will react to the outside, thinking hook block. Pass up the defensive end and drive hard upfield on the inside safety. The release is an influence technique to set up the end defender for the trap block of the backside guard. If aligned to the split end side, drive block the first defender to the inside. Should the defender slant inside, level off on the pursuing linebacker. Diagram 4-11 shows the defensive tackle slanting inside and the halfback blocking the flowing linebacker.

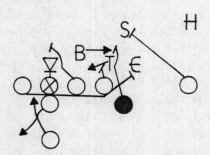

Diagram 4-11

Fullback—Fake the Buck Dive. Fill over the area of the pulling guard. Make a good enough fake so that the linebacker makes a tackle, taking himself out of the pursuit.

Backside halfback—Go in "fly" motion as in the Buck Dive and
Trap, on the snap drive for the original position of the
fullback. Receive the hand-off from the quarterback on
the second step. Drive hard through the fullback's position. Turn upfield and cut on the block of the pulling
guard. Cross the line of scrimmage with the shoulders
square to the goal line. Accelerate downfield and cut on
the block of the playside end (if running to a split end
formation) or playside halfback (if running to a tight end
formation).
Quarterback—Fake the Buck Dive to the fullback. Step back and
hand the ball to the motion back. Fake the bootleg after
the hand-off.

Diagram 4-12 shows the off-tackle play being run to the split end
side of the Double Slot formation. The playside halfback blocks the first
defender to his inside. In 4-12 the play is run at a 4-3 defense, the
playside halfback blocks the defensive end and the split end drives inside
for the safety.

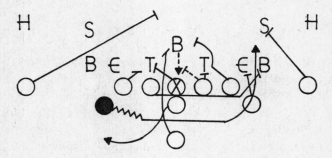

Diagram 4-12

In diagram 4-13 the play is run at an alignment variation in the 4-4
defense. This situation features the defensive tackles aligning in the guard
center gaps while the linebackers move outside on the outside shoulders
of the offensive guards.

KEY COACHING POINTS FOR THE OFF-TACKLE PLAY

1) The fullback and quarterback must carry out excellent fakes of
the Buck Dive (fullback) and Bootleg (quarterback).
2) If run to the split end side, the playside halfback will block the
first defender to his inside.

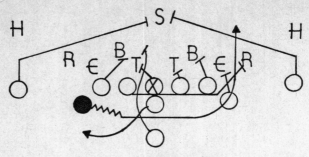

Diagram 4-13

3) The halfback will release tight through the outside hip of the defensive end when running the off-tackle to the tight end side. This helps the guard with his trap block and sets up the defensive end for the outside sweep.
4) The fullback will block the backside linebacker, removing the defender from pursuit of the play.
5) The backside tackle must work inside and fill the area of the pulling guard.

BUCK SWEEP

The Buck Sweep features all the same backfield actions of the Buck and Off-tackle plays. Emphasis must again be placed on carrying out fakes. On the Sweep both guards will pull. The techniques of the playside halfback and tight end are critical. Depending on the blocks of the playside halfback, tight end, and playside guard, the ball carrier will have an option to run inside or outside. Diagram 4-14 shows the Buck Sweep attacking a 5-2 defense.

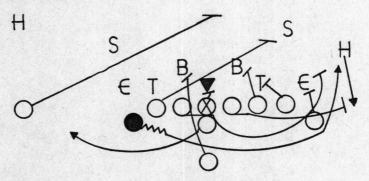

Diagram 4-14

TECHNIQUES FOR THE BUCK SWEEP

Playside end—If split, drive inside on the first defender on the line of scrimmage. If tight, drive block the first defender to the inside. If "flexed," split 4-6 yards and block the first defender inside on the line of scrimmage. The "flex" position is a short split by the tight end designed to obtain a flanking position on the defensive end. Diagram 4-15 shows the "flexed" tight end against the 4-4 defense.

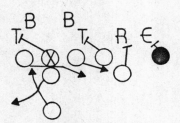

Diagram 4-15

Playside tackle—Block the first defender inside on or off the line of scrimmage. The "combo" call with the tight end can be used against the 5-2 defense. Because the playside guard will be pulling, the "combo" and "step" calls with the guard are not used.

Playside guard—Pull and gain depth of 2 yards. Block out on the first defender outside the playside halfback's block. When to the tight end side the guard will kick out on the defensive halfback coming up hard to the outside to contain the play.

Center—Drive block the first defender backside. No defender backside, block the defender aligned head on (middle guard).

Backside guard-Pull playside and wall-off to the inside. Pull shallow for two steps to clear the quarterback. Gain depth in an "arc" path to avoid defensive penetration. Check the block of the playside halfback before sealing off pursuit.

Backside tackle—Release inside the #2 defender. Work shallow across the field and get ahead of the play.

Backside end—If split or tight, release shallow and block the middle 1/3.

Playside halfback—If to the split end side, drive block the first defender to the inside. If the tight end is "flexed" align in the slot and block the first defender to the inside. If the end lines up tight, align in a "wing" position (one yard outside and one yard off the line from the tight end); drive block the first defender to the inside. When in the "wing" position the halfback must not let the defender get into the backfield and force the sweep deep.

Backside halfback—Go in motion. Receive the hand-off and run the sweep. Cut on the blocks of the tight end, playside halfback and backside guard.

Fullback—Fake the Buck Dive and block off the pursuit of the backside linebacker.

Quarterback—Fake the Buck Dive. Hand the ball to the motion man and carry out a bootleg fake to the backside.

KEY COACHING POINTS FOR THE SWEEP

1) Fakes of the other play dimensions must be carried out.
2) The playside guard will block the first defender outside the block of the playside halfback.
3) In the "flex" position the tight end attempts to outflank the end defender on the line of scrimmage. From the "flex" position the tight end will block the first defender inside on the line of scrimmage.
4) The playside halfback must hook block the defensive end to the inside when running the sweep to the tight end side.

Diagram 4-16 shows the Sweep being run to the split end side. The important blocks here are those of the playside halfback (blocking the first defender inside) and the playside guard.

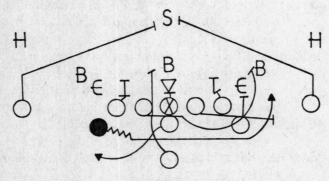

Diagram 4-16

The same Sweep play is run into a "flexed" end in diagram 4-17. The tight end takes a short split and outflanks the defensive end. On the snap the tight end will drive block on the first defender to the inside. The pulling playside guard will kick out on the defensive halfback.

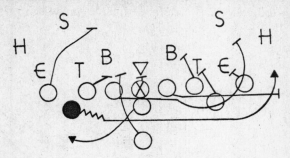

Diagram 4-17

BOOTLEG SWEEP (QUARTERBACK SWEEP)

As the final play in this series, the quarterback Sweep is presented. On this play the quarterback fakes the Buck Dive, the Sweep (off-tackle) and keeps the ball on his own sweep action. Both guards pull opposite the flow of the backfield. The flow of the backfield should get the defense into a pursuit course away from the run direction of the quarterback. This is quite an effective play against defenses that overshift in the direction of motion or pre-rotate their secondary to the motion side. Diagram 4-18 shows the defense pre-rotating in the direction of motion and the defense reacting to the backfield flow. A good block by the split end and playside

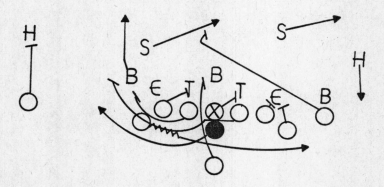

Diagram 4-18

guard should get the quarterback around the corner in good shape. To establish the maximum deception the quarterback must make two excellent fakes to the fullback and motioning halfback. In diagram 4-19, the Bootleg play is illustrated to the tight end side. The blocking assignment for the tight end is to block the first defender inside on the line of scrimmage.

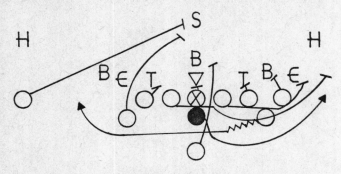

Diagram 4-19

NAMING THE BUCK SERIES PLAYS

1) The Buck Dive—To the left, "35 Buck Dive Left."
   To the right, "35 Buck Dive Right."
2) The Buck Trap—To the left, "36 Fullback Buck Trap."
   To the right, "34 Fullback Buck Trap."
3) The Buck Sweep—To the left "41 Buck Sweep."
   To the right, "19 Buck Sweep."
4) The Buck Off-Tackle—To the left, "42 Buck Off-Tackle."
   To the right, "18 Buck Off-Tackle."
5) The Bootleg Sweep—To the left, "21 Bootleg."
   To the right, "29 Bootleg."

5

Coaching Special Double Slot Option Plays

The running plays in this chapter once again stress the option game. The Double Slot formation is one of the most effective at controlling defensive pursuit, thus enhancing the potential of option plays. Only two basic option plays will be developed. Neither of these plays contain any initial ride fake to the fullback or halfbacks. The play action features a direct option technique by the quarterback. Initial action by the quarterback shows pass to the defense, while other members of the offense also show pass, giving the defense this sort of read. The offense attacks the areas vacated by defenders who have dropped off into pass coverage.

All the blocking up front will be basic rule. Common blocking calls can also be applied, depending on the defenses encountered.

STRAIGHT OPTION

Sprint out pass action is the key to establishing an initial look for this play action. The following areas of the offense must display pass to enhance the effectiveness of this play.

1) The quarterback shows a sprint out pass for two steps.
2) The ends and playside halfback show a pass release and drive the defenders covering them deep while maintaining the correct blocking position.
3) The fullback initiates sprint out pass protection steps and then leads up inside the defensive end, looking to seal off the defensive pursuit.
4) All backside interior linemen execute pass protection.

Diagram 5-1 shows the Straight Option. Assignments are as follows:

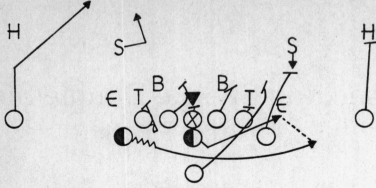

Diagram 5-1

Playside halfback—"arc" or "lead" on the pitch support.

Playside end—Release and block the defensive halfback.

Playside guard and tackle—Block rule. Apply calls as defense dictates.

Center—Block rule. Apply calls.

Backside guard—Pass block the #1 defender on the line of scrimmage.

Backside tackle—Pass block #2 on the line of scrimmage. If #2 is aligned to the inside, drive block the defender.

Backside end—Run a Post and draw the attention of the middle safety. If the safety is not drawn to the post he will outnumber the play as the option develops.

Backside halfback—Go in "fly" motion. Drive hard for the sideline, establishing the proper pitch relationship with the quarterback.

Fullback—Drive for the outside leg of the offensive tackle. If the defensive tackle is sliding to the outside, block the defender along with the offensive tackle. Should the defender be blocked, slide past and look immediately to the inside for a pursuing linebacker. The fullback takes initial steps the same as for his blocking on the sprint out pass. He does not attack the defensive end. Instead he cuts up inside and seals off inside-out pursuit. This gives the quarterback a pure option on the end defender.

Quarterback—Execute the sprint out pass for two steps. Slide down the line and react to the defensive end.

    1) If the defensive end plays quarterback, pitch the ball.

2) Should the defender move to the outside (or into the backfield), turn straight upfield with the ball.

USING THE STRAIGHT OPTION
AGAINST DEFENSIVE ALIGNMENT VARIATIONS

Diagram 5-2 illustrates a slanting 5-2 defense. In this situation the defense is slanting away from the motion while the linebackers are flowing towards it. The problem is having the playside guard make an effective block on the linebacker (the guard's assignment is the #1 defender). Because the linebacker is flowing fast, the defender could get to the quarterback before the guard could block him. To counter this defensive stunt "loop" blocking is used. "A" blocking is used by the backside guard and center.

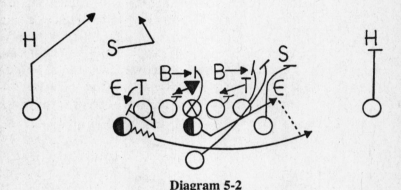

Diagram 5-2

FULLBACK OPTION

Diagram 5-3 shows the Fullback Option against the 4-4 defense. "Jet" motion is used as the play is run into the motion side. As the halfback develops his motion, the outside linebacker drops off with him. The defender keeps an inside-out position on the motion back so that any inside routes by the halfback will be covered. The halfback blocks the linebacker from outside-in. The split end releases and blocks the defender in the deep outside 1/3.

ASSIGNMENTS FOR THE FULLBACK OPTION

Playside end—If split and "jet" motion are used, slow block the defender in the deep outside 1/3. Should the defense ad-

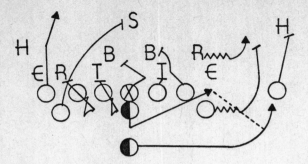

Diagram 5-3

just with corner rotation (the defensive halfback takes the flat while the safety covers the deep outside), pass up the rotating halfback and go after the safety, revolving to the deep outside 1/3. This situation is illustrated in diagram 5-4. If the secondary does not react to "jet," assume that the coverage is either corner rotation or man-to-man. React by driving past the shallow defender and work free in the deep outside 1/3. There is a pass play that takes advantage of man-to-man coverage and/or corner force.

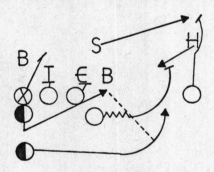

Diagram 5-4

If aligned as a tight end (and "jet" motion is used), release outside and drive for the deep 1/3. This technique is shown in diagram 5-5. In this situation, the defensive halfback adjusts to the outside and covers the motion man in man-to-man coverage. The safety now moves to cover the tight end also in man-to-man. The tight end uses an outside release and runs a bending course away from the

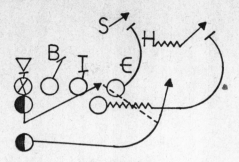

Diagram 5-5

safety. This technique sets up the correct blocking position or puts the tight end in a wide open situation, should the safety decide to react quickly towards the line of scrimmage.

Playside guard and tackle—Block rule. Use calls.

Center—Block rule. Use calls.

Backside guard—Pass block #1 on line. If "A" call, block middle guard.

Backside tackle—Pass block #2 on line. If "A" call is made, block #1 defender on line.

Backside end—Run the post.

Playside halfback—Execute "jet" motion. On the snap, drive for a position outside the defender covering the short flat. In a 4 deep, this defender will be the safety or halfback, depending on the type of rotation being used by the defense. When running the play to a tight end side, the playside halfback uses the same "jet" technique but finds that the defensive halfback now covers him man-to-man. If running at a 4 deep secondary, the safety covers the tight end man-to-man. Should the defensive alignment be an 8-man front, then the outside linebacker locks on the tight end man-to-man. When motioning to a tight end side, the playside halfback will drive the defensive halfback into the outside 1/3 zone. This technique is illustrated in diagram 5-5.

Fullback—Open to the playside with a cross-over step. Work for the correct pitch relationship with the quarterback.

Backside halfback—Release shallow to the inside. Work across field and get ahead of the play. Block the middle safety.

> **Quarterback**—Fake a quick dropback pass for two steps. Slide down the line and option the defensive end. The two drop steps aid the fullback in establishing the correct pitch relationship.

FULLBACK OPTION WITH "JET" MOTION

Diagram 5-6 shows the use of extended "jet" motion. This technique places the motioning halfback outside the split end. The extended motion is used only towards a split end. On the snap the playside halfback drives deep and blocks the outside 1/3. The split end is now responsible for blocking in the flat area. In 5-6 the play is run at a 4-4 defense. The outside linebacker drops off with motion to a point where he can cover inside routes and get into the throwing lane on out patterns. As a result the linebacker "chases" the motion but not outside the split end. The "backer" will now cover the split end on inside patterns and the defensive halfback will cover the motion man in the deep outside 1/3. On the snap, the split end will draw the linebacker to the inside, gaining some depth. The end blocks the linebacker when the defender reacts to run action. To make the play really effective, the offense must again fake pass as in the Straight Option play.

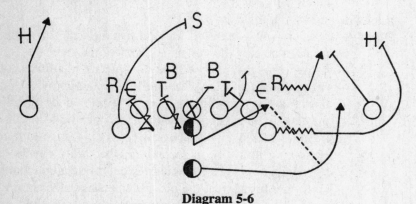

Diagram 5-6

Diagram 5-7 shows the Fullback Option play being run away from the "jet" motion side. If the defense is really worried about the pass and starts rotating the middle safety, then the offense can begin to successfully attack the backside of the formation. In the diagram a 4-deep secondary starts running its safety to the deep middle to be in a position to outnumber the run and help on the coverage to the motion side. The quarterback then runs the play back away from the motion and secondary rota-

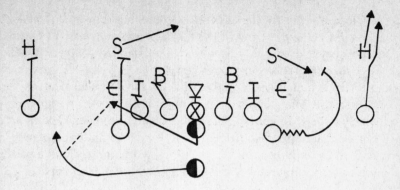

Diagram 5-7

tion. Blocking downfield takes place by the halfback and split end to the side away from motion. The split end blocks the deep outside 1/3. The offensive halfback blocks the pitch support (defender responsible for the pitchman), releasing and using "lead" blocking techniques. All interior blocking remains rule with special calls to be made. The quarterback and fullback execute the same techniques but away from the motion side.

"Fly" motion can also be utilized when running the Fullback Option. Diagram 5-8 shows the play with "fly" motion technique by the halfback. The defensive secondary shows pre-rotation as the halfback starts in motion. Unless the motion man can get ahead of the fullback, the play loses the advantage of an extra lead blocker. Should the defense pre-rotate as shown, then it can outnumber the offense to the playside. The motion back just does not end up in good position to become an effective lead blocker. The offense may incorporate an extension of the "fly" motion as shown in the diagram. This places the halfback in a position to

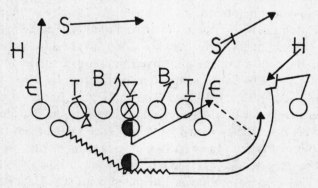

Diagram 5-8

become a lead blocker for the fullback. On the motion signal the backside halfback starts in the direction of the fullback and goes behind him working to the playside of the formation. The ball is snapped when the backside halfback motions to a point behind the playside offensive tackle. The motion man then helps with the block on the defender responsible for the pitch support. The extended "fly" motion fits in well with the play as it frequently is used in certain pass plays off the Fullback Option action. Blocking assignments for the interior line remain unchanged. The playside halfback will use the "lead" block with emphasis on a pass pattern release. The split end will continue to block the deep outside 1/3 defender.

In diagram 5-9 the same "fly" motion is shown with the Fullback Option being run away from the motion direction.

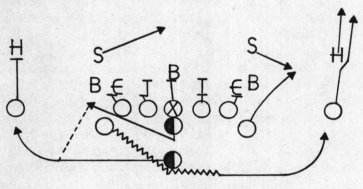

Diagram 5-9

"Motion" is the most effective technique in forcing the defense to show an adjustment before the snap. Diagram 5-10 shows "motion" with the Fullback Option being run in the same direction. The defense is playing a 4 deep secondary. On "motion" one of the safeties chases the halfback all the way across the offensive formation. Remaining defenders play man-to-man. The ball is snapped as the motion back just passes the position of the playside halfback. The motioning halfback blocks the pitch support defender. The motion man drives into the flat, drawing the defender with him; the motion man blocks the safety from outside in. Both the split end and playside halfback block their regular assignments; the end—the deep outside 1/3; the halfback using a "lead" technique.

In 5-11 the same motion is illustrated with the 4 deep defenders using a zone coverage to the motion side. In this situation the playside safety runs into the flat, covering the motion man (or split end should he run a short pattern and the motion man drive deep); the defensive halfback "zones" the deep outside 1/3. The backside safety rotates to the deep middle, watching for the release of the playside halfback. All blocking assignments remain the same; the split end takes the deep outside 1/3 while the motion man blocks the flat. A good release and "lead" technique by the playside halfback should occupy the backside safety and keep him from the play.

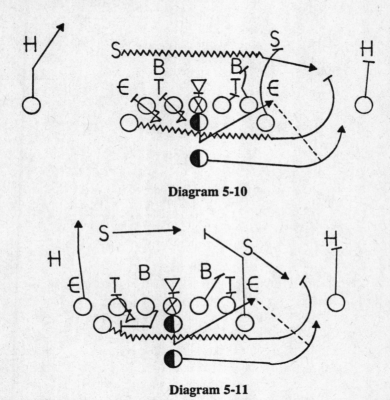

Diagram 5-10

Diagram 5-11

Diagram 5-12 shows the play run at the 4-4 defense that adjusts by dropping off an outside linebacker in the direction of motion. The linebacker covers the flat and is blocked by the motion man. The end fakes a deep pass route and blocks the defensive halfback, while the playside halfback releases on a "lead" block at the middle safety.

Against a 3-deep secondary and running the Fullback Option to the tight end side creates the situation illustrated in diagram 5-13. Here the outside linebacker plays the tight end man-to-man. The middle safety slides over and covers the playside halfback, also man-to-man. As the motion man works outside the tight end, he is picked up man-to-man by

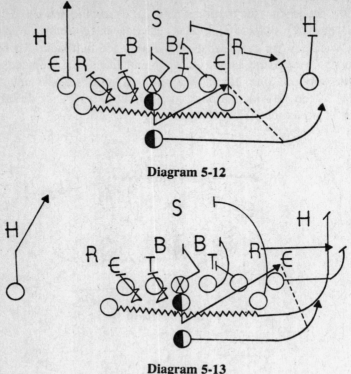

Diagram 5-12

Diagram 5-13

the defensive halfback. In this situation the tight end uses an outside release and draws the linebacker into the flat. The motion man drives deep,
taking the defensive halfback with him. The playside halfback will release and run the "lead" block on the safety.

The Fullback Option can also be effectively run to the backside
away from motion. In diagram 5-14 the play is run backside at an adjusted
5-2 defense. The defense compensates for the motion by moving the
backside safety in the direction of motion and covers the halfback man-
to-man. The safety and defensive halfback to the motion side play zone
defense. The defensive line adjusts by sliding down 1/2 man in the direction of the motion. Because of the closeness of the defensive end, the
quarterback must be ready to pitch the ball quickly to the fullback.

Diagram 5-15 shows the Fullback Option being run away from motion but against an 8-man front defense (4-4). Special blocking by the
playside tackle is used. The offensive tackle pulls to the outside and
blocks the linebacker. As motion develops, the backside linebacker
"walks off" and cushions the hook zone underneath the split end. Be-

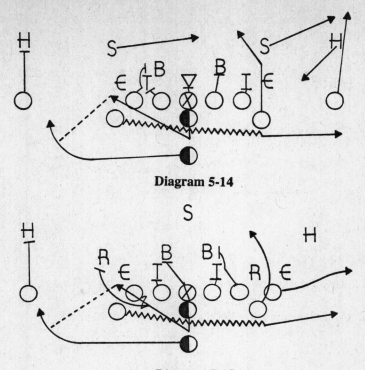

Diagram 5-14

Diagram 5-15

cause of this position the defense now outnumbers the offensive play to this side. The alignment of the defensive end allows him easy penetration into the offensive backfield. The quick penetration forces the quarterback to pitch the ball almost instantly after the drop back pass fake. Because of the quick delivery from the quarterback, the fullback is not in a good position for the pitch relationship. As a result the dropped off linebacker, once he reads run, has sufficient time to recover and tackle the fullback at the line of scrimmage. This is the primary reason why the tackle pulls and blocks the linebacker. Actually the tackle executes a screen pass block technique. The tackle pass blocks for two counts (showing pass to the outside linebacker), then releases to the outside attacking the linebacker. By pass blocking the defensive end, the tackle delays the defender from getting to the quarterback too quickly. This delay provides the proper timing and makes the option read more effective.

A switch in blocking assignments can take place between the tackle and split end. This is especially effective near the goal line where the defense is operating at a minimum depth. The split end drives to the inside and blocks the linebacker, while the tackle pass blocks two counts and blocks the defensive corner back. This blocking scheme is illustrated in diagram 5-16.

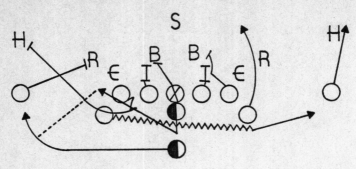

Diagram 5-16

NAMING THE PLAYS

1) Straight Option—To the right, "19 Straight Option."
    To the left, "41 Straight Option."
2) Fullback Option—To the right, "39 Fullback Option."
    To the left, "31 Fullback Option."

6

Coaching the Double Slot Belly Series

The Belly series is also developed around the fullback as the primary ball carrier. Play actions will vary somewhat from the Veer series, but all will continue to feature a ride fake between the quarterback and fullback. The first play in the series is the Outside Belly, which directs the fullback at a running lane off the outside leg of the offensive tackle.

Next in the series is the natural extension of the Belly play, the Belly Option. Here is still another example of the use of the Double Slot as the basis for an option-oriented attack. The Outside Belly and Belly Option work primarily on the defensive end, forcing him to play the fullback on the Belly or the quarterback on the option. First the Outside Belly play is run to get the defensive end to start to close down and shut off the fullback. Once this occurs, the offense attacks outside with the Belly Option.

A trap play with a pulling guard as the primary blocker is presented next. The trap play is based on the action of the Outside Belly play. The ball is faked to the fullback then handed back to the motioning halfback who cuts on the block of the trapping guard. This play is called the Belly Handback Trap.

The Belly Counter is a play designed to take advantage of defensive pursuit. In this play the Belly Action is faked to the fullback. The ball is then handed off to the halfback, who follows the trap blocking guard to the backside.

The last play in the series is another counter action featuring the use of the tackle as a trap blocker. This Belly Counter Tackle Trap will be directly related to the Fullback Outside Belly but there will be no ride fake by the quarterback. The quarterback uses a deep reverse pivot and hand-off to the stationary halfback (the one not going in motion), who will follow and cut upfield on the block of the pulling tackle. The fullback runs the Outside Belly over the tackle's position, fill blocking for the pulling offensive lineman.

OUTSIDE BELLY

Diagram 6-1 shows the Outside Belly play being run into a tight end formation. All line blocking consists of the application of basic rules and variation calls as the defensive situation dictates. Assignments are as follows:

Playside end—If tight, block the end man on the line of scrimmage (first defender aligned to the outside). If split, drive inside and block the safety or outside linebacker depending on the defense.

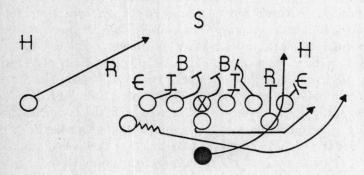

Diagram 6-1

Playside linemen—Block Veer with adjustment calls.
Center—Block Veer with adjustment calls.
Backside linemen—Block Veer with adjustments.
Backside end—Release shallow and run a post pattern.
Playside halfback—Against a 7 man front (5-2 and 4-3 type defenses) "combo" block with the offensive tackle and then "lead" on the near safety. Against 8 man fronts (4-4 and 5-3 type alignments) drive block #3.
Backside halfback—Execute the same techniques as in the Veer play.
Fullback—Open to the playside with a cross-over step. Drive for the outside leg of the offensive tackle. Receive the

hand-off and cut on the blocks of the tight end, playside halfback and offensive tackle.

Quarterback—Reverse pivot and step to a point 3 yards behind the offensive tackle. Place the ball in the fullback's pocket and watch the reactions of the defensive end. Give the ball to the fullback and accelerate a fake to the outside.

The use of "jet" motion is illustrated in diagram 6-2. This motion is used on the side of the formation away from the play direction. The offense loses the fake option dimension of the play, but the quarterback continues his fake to the outside. By using "jet," the defense may suspect a Fullback Option play and rotate to the motion as a compensating adjustment.

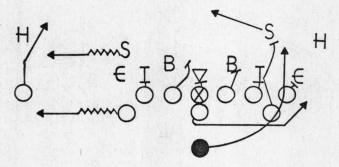

Diagram 6-2

Several blocking adjustments and variations can be used when running the Outside Belly play. In diagram 6-3 a simple cross block between the tight end and the halfback is illustrated. In this situation the tight end drives inside on the first defender. The halfback delays and allows the

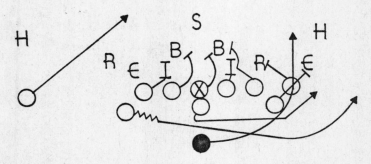

Diagram 6-3

tight end to clear, he then blocks out on the defensive end. The play is
being run at a 4-4 defense. A "combo" block is used by the playside
guard and tackle to seal off the inside two defenders.

Diagram 6-4 shows the use of "G" blocking. This scheme was used
also as an alternate in running the Halfback Slant play in the Veer series.
A stack 5-2 defense is being attacked. Both the tight end and tackle drive
block the first defender to their inside. The playside halfback lets the tight
end clear, then drives across the line "leading" on the safety.

"Motion" is used to force a defensive rotation adjustment as shown
in diagram 6-5. The Belly play is directed opposite the "motion" with
"G" blocking by the linemen.

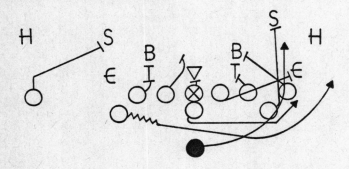

Diagram 6-4

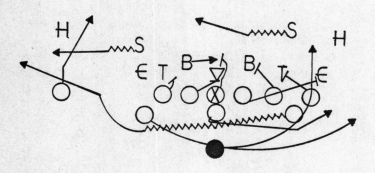

Diagram 6-5

BELLY OPTION

The Belly Option is an extension of the Outside Belly play. In this
action the ball is directed to the outside off an option read by the quarter-

back. All techniques of the Outside Belly play are featured but the ball is definitely being taken to the defensive perimeter. Diagram 6-6 shows the play run at the 5-2 defense. Blocking schemes will be the same as those for the Veer option.

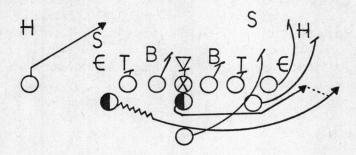

Diagram 6-6

BELLY HANDBACK TRAP

The Belly Trap play is depicted in diagram 6-7. Line blocking is based on the long trap concept. Because of the need required by trap blocking, the play is best run into a tight end formation. Key positions and their techniques are as follows:

Playside halfback—Drive through the outside leg of the defender to be trapped. Against 7-man fronts (5-2 and 4-3 alignments) this will be the defender opposite the playside tackle. In 8-man fronts (4-4 and 5-3 schemes) this will be the outside linebacker or the defender aligning over the playside halfback. By driving through the outside leg of

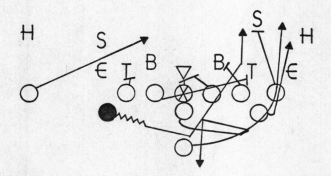

Diagram 6-7

the defender a false pressure situation is created. Since the defender is coached to fight pressure, the halfback blocking down for a short count gets the defender to react to the outside, making the trap block by the guard easier. After working through the outside leg, the halfback will release pressure and attack the safety.

Fullback—Run the Outside Belly play. Attempt to draw the defender to be trapped to the outside.

Quarterback—Reverse pivot and fake the Outside Belly to the fullback. Disconnect the ball and pivot back to the inside handing the ball to the backside halfback. After the handoff drop back and set up faking a pass.

Backside halfback—Use "fly" motion. Drive through the original position of the fullback. Cut up hard receiving the ball from the quarterback. Key the block of the pulling backside guard.

BELLY COUNTER

This play features belly action to the fullback with misdirection in the backfield. The fullback's direction is now more towards the outside hip of the backside guard. The hand-off is made to the stationary backside halfback. Long trap blocking is the featured scheme and the play is shown in diagram 6-8.

SPECIAL TECHNIQUES FOR THE BELLY COUNTER

Quarterback—Reverse pivot but not as deep as the Outside Belly play. As the pivot is made, the ball is placed on the quarterback's stomach. A one handed fake is made to the fullback. The ball is handed off with the hand opposite the fake. (*Note:* This is the right hand when the play is directed to the left side of the formation.)

Fullback—Lead step at the outside foot of the backside guard. Make a good fake over the ball and fill for the pulling lineman. The path is run tighter than on the Outside Belly.

Playside halfback—Go in "fly" motion and fake the option play to the backside.

Backside halfback—Drop step with the inside foot. Drive back,

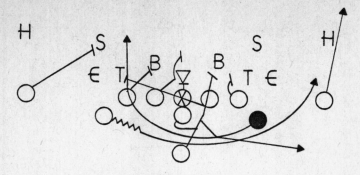

Diagram 6-8

aiming for the original position of the fullback. Receive
the ball from the quarterback and cut on the block of the
pulling guard.

Playside end—Line Up tight. Block the first linebacker inside.

Playside tackle—Block the first defender inside on the line of
scrimmage. Should the inside defender be inside the
playside guard, then block the first linebacker inside.

Playside guard—The guard will look first for a defensive player
inside (on the offensive center). If there is no defender
inside that is on the line of scrimmage, then the guard
will block the defender lined up head on.

Center—The center must first check the backside, if there is no defender on the guard then he will block the man on. If
there is no man backside or no man on then the center
will block the linebacker over.

Backside guard—Pull and block the first defender past the block of
the playside guard.

Backside tackle—Fill block over the position of the pulling guard.

Backside end—Release and block the middle 1/3.

In diagram 6-9 "motion" is used directing the playside halfback all
the way across the formation. As the defense pre-rotates and goes into
man-to-man coverage, it is hit with the Belly Counter play going back
away from the motion. Once again the play is directed to the tight end
side of the formation.

The Belly Counter can be run back away from a tight end to the split
side of the formation. Diagram 6-10 illustrates this situation. A 5-2 defense rotates its secondary on "fly" motion and initial ball action. The
effectiveness of the play depends a great deal on how the defense reacts to

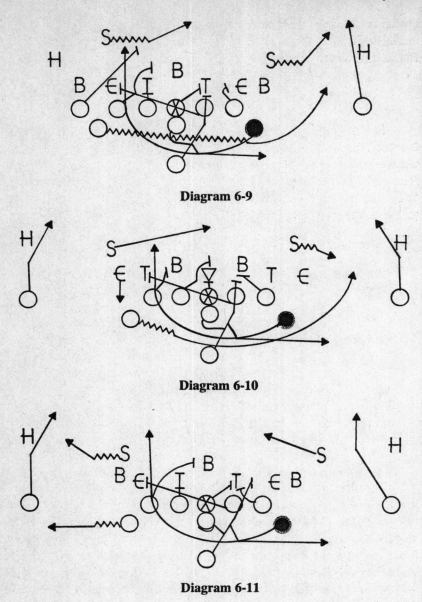

Diagram 6-9

Diagram 6-10

Diagram 6-11

the motion and initial ball action. Because the backside safety rotates to the deep middle and the defensive end has penetrated into backfield, the counter action has an excellent chance.

Using "jet" motion into a split end and running the counter to that side is shown in diagram 6-11. A Pro 4-3 defense is being attacked. The playside safety adjusts to the "jet" action by revolving to the flat. On the backside, the safety starts to rotate to the deep middle but is held up by the initial ball fake. With the secondary reacting this way, the play has a sound chance of gaining considerable yardage.

COUNTER TRACKLE TRAP

The Counter Tackle Trap is another counter action getting the ball to the stationary halfback off the fake of the Outside Belly play. Trapping is done by an offensive tackle instead of a guard. For the quarterback the footwork is the same as for the Outside Belly. There is no fake to the fullback; the quarterback uses a deep reverse pivot and hands the ball off to the halfback. The ball carrier follows and cuts on the block of the trapping tackle. The fullback runs the Belly course filling over the outside leg of the offensive tackle.

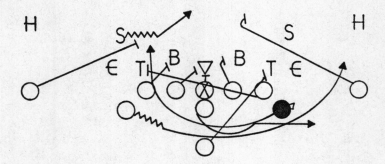

Diagram 6-12

Strategically the play is used against defenses that start flowing their inside linebackers to stop the Outside Belly play. The linebackers are put into a conflict in their reactions. Should they flow fast to cover the Outside Belly, the blocking angles are very easy for the line. If they stay at home looking for the Counter action, then the Outside Belly should be that more effective. Generally, if they flow fast, they are vulnerable to the Counter; if reading for the Counter play, they lose their effectiveness on pursuit to stop the Outside Belly play. Because of the play's design, a number of motion patterns can be utilized.

Diagram 6-12 illustrates the Counter Tackle Trap against the 5-2 defense. Individual assignments and techniques are as follows:

Playside end—If split, release and block the deep middle 1/3. Against a 3 deep, block the middle safety. Against a 4 deep the block will be on the first inside safety. If tight, block the defender aligned in the head on position. Should there be no defender in the head on position, drive block the first linebacker to the inside.

Playside tackle—Drive block the first defender to the inside on the line of scrimmage. If the inside defender is over the offensive center, then drive block the first linebacker to the inside.

Playside guard—Drive block the first defender inside on the line of scrimmage. If there is no defender inside as in the 4-3 defense, then block the defender aligned head on.

Center—Block the first defender to the backside that is on the line of scrimmage. If the backside down lineman is wider than the backside guard, then block the man on (middle guard). The backside blocking rule would be used against the 4-3 and Wide Tackle 6 defenses; while the "on" rule would be used vs. the 5-2 and 5-3 defenses. The 4-4 requires specific techniques and is covered under a separate heading.

Backside Guard—Fill block the area of the pulling tackle.

Backside tackle—Pull and trap the first defender beyond the offensive center. Actually the tackle traps the first defender outside the playside offensive guard.

Backside end—If split, release and block the near safety (middle 1/3.) If tight, cut off the first defender over the first man to the inside.

Playside halfback—Go in "fly" motion and fake the option play.

Backside halfback—Jab step to the outside to establish the correct timing. Drop step with the inside foot and gain depth to 2 yards behind the original position of the offensive tackle. Receive the ball from the quarterback and look for the block by the pulling tackle. Cut upfield with the shoulders square to the line of scrimmage.

Fullback—Open step at the inside foot of the trapping tackle. Run a direct path to this point and fill block.

Quarterback—Reverse pivot and gain depth (3 yards). Allow the fullback to clear. Make an inside hand-off to the halfback. After the hand-off continue to the outside faking the Belly Option play.

COUNTER TACKLE TRAP VS. THE 4-4 DEFENSE

The 4-4 defense is a very effective alignment against a trapping game. A team that features the middle trap action in its running attack finds itself being outnumbered over the area of the offensive center and guards. Because of this outnumbering, the offense must change some of its blocking rules and techniques. The 4-4 defense does require the teaching of special blocking schemes because of the alignment of individual defenders and the various areas of their responsibility.

The Counter Tackle Trap is no exception, and certain assignments for offensive linemen must be modified when facing this defense. The Tackle Trap blocking scheme, however, is one of the most effective against this defense. A guard trap scheme can be utilized (see Fullback Buck Trap) but with only a limited degree of success.

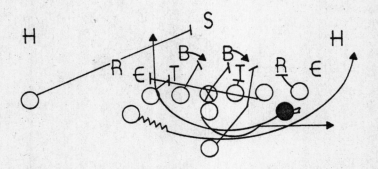

Diagram 6-13

The Tackle Trap is illustrated in diagram 6-13 against the 4-4 defense. Against this alignment the offense takes advantage of the pursuit of the 2 inside linebackers. A good fake by the fullback will draw the pursuit of the linebackers in the direction of the initial offensive flow. The quarterback mades this fake more effective with his reverse pivot as in the Outside Belly play. The initial movements of the offense must show the Outside Belly to the defense. As the linebackers flow, the inside linebacker to the side of the fake will scrape to the outside, thinking the play is the Outside Belly. The same inside linebacker will be more effectively drawn as the center will also step in the direction of the fake. This is the correct read for the inside linebacker (center and backs flow, scrape for the fullback). If the center blocked to the backside (away from the

play fake) then the linebacker would fill quickly and disrupt the timing of
the play.

As the play develops, the center cuts off the pursuit of this
linebacker back in the direction of the trapping tackle. The other inside
linebacker (the one on the actual playside) is also given a "false read."
The offensive center steps to the fake side (his regular technique on the
Belly play vs. the 4-4 defense) while the playside guard is stepping this
way also. If the linebacker is reading his key correctly (guard to fullback)
he should scrape to protect the middle. This gives the playside guard the
correct blocking angle to cut off the backer's pursuit to the playside. The

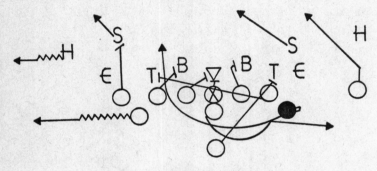

Diagram 6-14

playside offensive tackle will block the first defender to the inside on the
line of scrimmage. As the trapping tackle pulls, he will look first to trap
the defender outside the block of the playside tackle. Should the defender
penetrate into the backfield, the pulling tackle will turn upfield and lead
the play. All remaining techniques are unchanged. The adjustments
against the 4-4 take place in the line play and it is in the offensive line that
the false keys are established. Should the linebackers start "staying
home" or shooting the guard-center gaps, then the Outside Belly play
should develop very effectively.

Using "jet" and running the Counter Tackle Trap to a tight end side
is shown in diagram 6-14. The motion man draws the defensive halfback
to the outside and eventually to the deep 1/3 on the snap. The rule for the
playside tight end is to block the first linebacker to the inside. Because of
the "jet" motion to the tight end's side, he will release two steps inside,
then attack the safety from an inside-out angle. All remaining techniques
are unchanged.

NAMING THE BELLY SERIES PLAYS

1) The Outside Belly—To the right, "37 Outside Belly."
      To the left, "32 Outside Belly."
2) The Outside Belly Option—To the right, "19 Belly Option."
      To the left, "41 Belly Option."
3) The Belly Handback Trap—To the right, "16 Belly Handback Trap."
      To the left, "44 Belly Handback Trap."
4) The Belly Counter—To the right, "17 Belly Counter."
      To the Left, "43 Belly Counter."
5) The Counter Tackle Trap—To the right, "17 Counter Tackle Trap."
      To the left, "43 Counter Tackle Trap."

7

Coaching Complementary Double Slot Running Plays

The plays in this chapter are for the most part designed to stand alone. That is, in most cases they are not derivatives from one of the basic series already presented. First in the series of complementary plays is the End Around. This play is developed off the Veer Option action and features all the dimensions of the option with the quarterback pitching the ball to the split end coming back to the inside across the formation. The End Around to the tight end is developed in two phases, first as a pitch off the Veer action and second as a sweep off the Halfback Slant play. For the most part End Arounds can be categorized as Veer action plays. Briefly mentioned is the End Around off the Straight and Fullback Option actions.

Second in this play series is a Power Sweep with the fullback leading. The play differs from the Buck Sweep in that the fullback will lead the play and not fill for one of the pulling guards. A Reverse off this action with the halfback carrying serves as a complementary play against defenses that flow fast on the fullback and sweep movements.

END AROUND

Diagrams 7-1A and 7-1B show the End Around being run at an 8-man front (4-4 defense diagram 7-1A) and a 7-man front (5-2 defense diagram 7-1B). It is important that the Fullback Veer and Double Option plays be effectively faked. The pitch must be so timed that it looks as

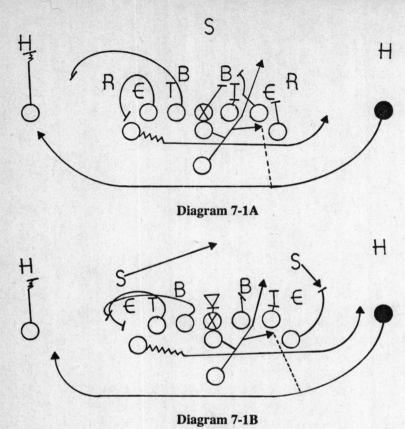

Diagram 7-1A

Diagram 7-1B

though the split end coming back around has intercepted it. The playside blocking must be worked on and emphasis must be placed on the proper techniques and assignments. Outlined below is the breakdown.

END AROUND ASSIGNMENTS AND TECHNIQUES

Playside end—If tight or split, release and drive deep into the outside 1/3 area. Watch the reactions of the defender and block him from outside-in when the defender reacts to the play.

Playside tackle—Step down to the inside as if releasing downfield. Gain depth at 2 yards and pull to the outside. "Peel" back and block the defensive end. Be sure to block above the waist and don't clip.

Playside guard—Use the same techniques as for the playside tackle. Pull back to the outside at a depth of 4 yards.

"Peel" block back on the defender coming across in pursuit at an approximate depth of 5 yards.

Center—Block the Veer.

Backside guard—Execute Veer blocking.

Backside tackle—Block the Veer Option. It is important that you try to hook the defender on you. This allows the quarterback more time to get outside and pitch the ball to the split end.

Backside end—Split 10 yards from the tackle. On the snap drop step back to the inside and come back across the offensive formation at a depth of approximately 7 yards. Look the pitch all the way in from the quarterback and sprint to the outside. Get by the contain defender (usually the defensive end) by keying the block of the playside tackle.

Playside halfback—Go in motion and fake the Veer Option to the backside.

Backside halfback—"Arc" or "lead" block on the backside perimeter. Drive block #3 if running against an 8 man front.

Fullback—Fake the Veer.

Quarterback—Execute the Veer fake. Disconnect the ball and accelerate down the line. Pitch the ball to the split end coming back to the inside. It is important that the timing on this play be such that it looks as though the split end has intercepted the pitch to the halfback.

In diagram 7-2 the End Around is being run back in the direction of the tight end. All assignments are unchanged. The tight end must release inside and drive to the outside working for leverage on the outside 1/3

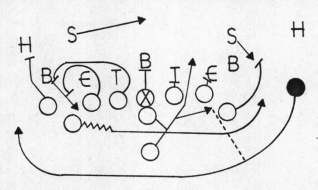

Diagram 7-2

defender. The end must watch for the defensive back to react and then block him to the inside.

The Straight Option action is shown in diagram 7-3. In this play action the quarterback does not initiate any inside fake to one of the running backs. He uses two quick drop steps and slides down the line optioning the defensive end. As the quarterback approaches the defensive end, he pitches the ball back to the split end. Again the timing must be such that it appears the split end has intercepted the ball.

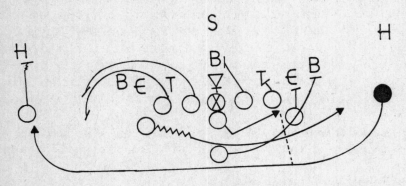

Diagram 7-3

Utilization of the Fullback Option action can also be run as an End Around play. Because of the backfield action, various motion types can be incorporated to establish a desired rotation or coverage effect from the defense. In diagram 7-4 "motion" is utilized and man-to-man secondary coverage is shown. The backside safety chases the motion man all the way across the formation. The fullback and quarterback fake the option down the line. The quarterback once again pitches the ball to the split end. "Jet" motion is illustrated in diagram 7-5. As the motion develops

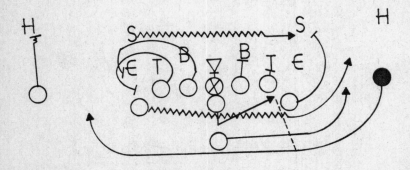

Diagram 7-4

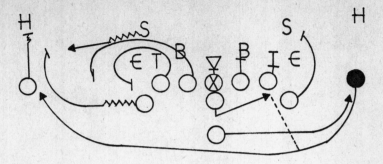

Diagram 7-5

the defensive secondary rotates in that direction. Two blockers are now in position to handle the secondary reactions. The end releases and blocks the deep 1/3 defender while the motion man takes the short flat defender. Against an 8-man front the defense drops off an outside linebacker to the "jet" side. This is shown in diagram 7-6. The tight end blocks the deep outside 1/3 while the motion man blocks the flat coverage.

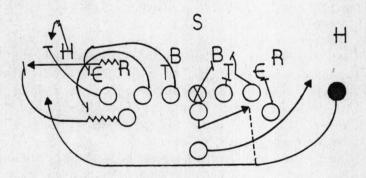

Diagram 7-6

In diagram 7-7 the tight end now receives the pitch. Because of the position of the tight end, the quarterback must deliver the ball sooner to the ball carrier. As soon as the ball is disconnected from the Veer fake to the fullback, the quarterback will deliver the pitch to the end. The pitch must be timed so that it appears as though the end has intercepted the pitch.

KEY COACHING POINTS FOR THE END AROUND

1) Playside ends must drive hard into the outside deep 1/3 and block the defensive halfback.
2) Good "peel" blocks by the playside offensive linemen. Timing

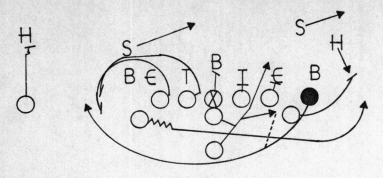

Diagram 7-7

and practice are essential for execution of the correct blocking technique.

3) The play action, whether it be Veer Option, Straight Option, or Fullback Option action, must be convincingly faked to get the flow by the defense in the desired directions.

4) Depending on the backfield action, various motion types can be used to control the defensive secondary to enhance the effectiveness of the play.

5) Different timing is required when running the End Around to the split end (when he becomes the ball carrier) or tight end. When running the ball to the split end around, the quarterback can execute the option fake dimension of the play almost all the way to the pitch-keep (defensive end) key. Should the tight end be designated as the ball carrier, the quarterback will deliver the ball on the second step into the option fake.

6) Practice and timing must be worked on so that it appears that the ball carrier has intercepted the pitch from the quarterback.

TIGHT END SWEEP

As a variation in utilizing the tight end as a ballcarrier, sweep action with the tight end carrying can also be used. In diagram 7-8 the Slant play is faked and the ball handed off to the end. The fullback fakes his Slant assignment, actually fill blocking for the pulling guard. Other dimensions of the Slant are carried out by the quarterback and halfback. As he rides the halfback into the line, the quarterback watches the tight end. When the end reaches a point where the halfback originally lines up, the quarterback disconnects the ball and hands it to the tight end coming back to the inside. To achieve the proper timing on the play, the tight end may

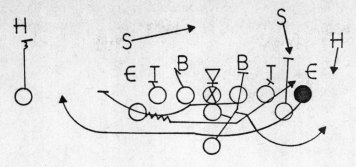

Diagram   8

take an extra foot split. The fakes by the quarterback must be quick but effective enough to get the defense flowing. As he pivots back, the tight end must stay tight to the slanting halfback to achieve maximum deception with the play action. The quarterback makes an outside hand-off. As he pulls, the guard must be flat for two steps, to clear the quarterback's footwork; he then must gain depth and overthrow on the defensive end. (*Overthrow block:* Pulling lineman attacks a defensive end and works his hips and shoulder past the outside hips of the defender.) The split end (or tight end depending upon the formation) blocks the deep outside 1/3. Against an 8-man front the end will drive block #3 if he aligns as a tight end, or screen block the outside linebacker if he aligns as a split end. Diagram 7-9 shows the Tight End Sweep against an 8-man front with the split end screening off to the inside.

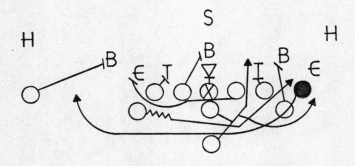

Diagram 7-9

KEY COACHING POINTS
FOR THE TIGHT END SWEEP

1) Excellent faking of the Slant play. Good rides by the quarterback and superb fill block by the fullback.

2) Good timing and an outside hand-off by the quarterback.
3) Slightly wider split (2 extra feet) by the tight end, to establish the correct hand-off timing.
4) Hard work by the pulling guard to overthrow the defensive end.
5) Good reading of the defense by the split end. Screen inside against an 8-man front (3 deep). Block deep outside vs. 7-man front (4-deep).

RUNNING THE TIGHT END SWEEP
AT DIFFERENT DEFENSIVE FRONTS

Diagrams 7-10 and 7-11 show examples of the Tight End Sweep being run at two defensive variations. First, in diagram 7-10 the play is being run at an overshifted 5-3 defense. Against this version of the 5-3 the split end must drive down inside on the linebacker. The end must be careful not to block below the defender's waist. The playside tackle must reach block the defensive end and attempt to turn the defender to the inside. As he pulls and reaches his blocking point, the guard will check the

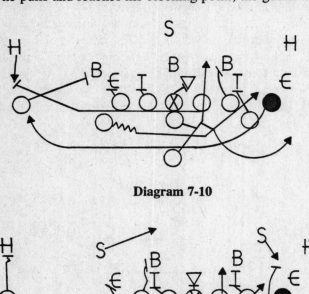

Diagram 7-10

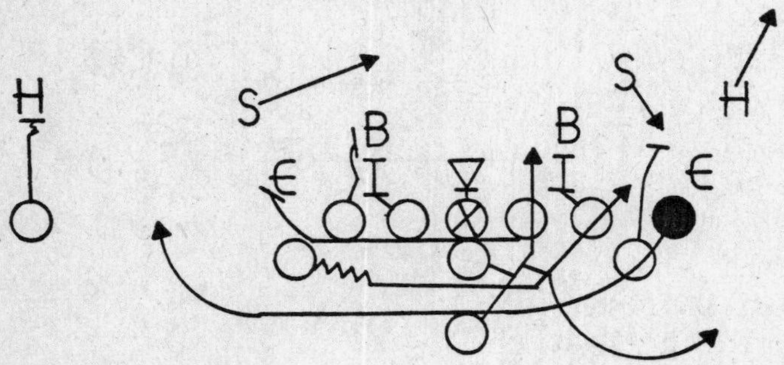

Diagram 7-11

blocks of the split end and playside tackle, helping each as the situation dictates.

In diagram 7-11 a 5-2 stack (7-man front, 4-deep) defense is illustrated. In this situation the playside guard and tackle execute a good "combo" block while the split end blocks the deep outside 1/3. (*Note:* Should the defensive secondary show an invert look to the split end side, then the end will screen block this defender to the inside.)

POWER SWEEP

The Power Sweep differs from the Buck Sweep in the backfield action. The Power Sweep has the fullback leading at the defensive end. Two play actions by the quarterback will be discussed. First, the quarterback will reverse pivot and pitch the ball back to the motioning halfback. After the pitch the quarterback will lead the play as one of the blockers. The second play action involves the quarterback using an open pivot and handing the ball off to the motion back. When the quarterback pitches the ball to the halfback, the ball carrier can gain some depth and read the blocks at the perimeter. Should the hand-off be made, the ball carrier will have to run a more shallow course. On the hand-off action the quarterback will carry out a bootleg fake. In diagrams 7-12A and 7-12B the Power Sweep is illustrated in two situations.

INDIVIDUAL ASSIGNMENTS AND
TECHNIQUES FOR THE POWER SWEEP

Essentially the assignments are the same as those for the Buck Sweep.

Playside end—If tight, drive down on the first defender to the inside. If split, drive to the inside and block the safetyman.

Playside tackle—Drive block the first defender inside.

Playside guard—Pull and drive the contain defender into the sidelines.

Center—Block the man on or backside.

Backside guard—Pull and lead the play downfield. Help playside halfback.

Backside tackle—Pull and fill the area vacated by the backside pulling guard.

Backside end—Release and block the middle deep 1/3.

Playside Halfback—Attack the outside thigh of the defensive end.

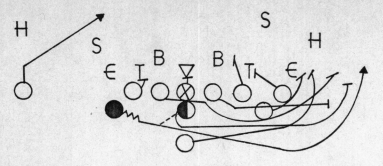

Diagram 7-12A

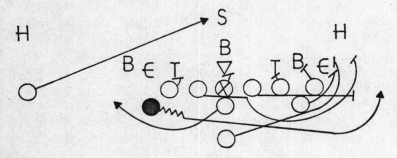

Diagram 7-12B

Hook the defender to the inside.

Fullback—Lead step at the defensive end and help the playside halfback with his block.

Backside halfback—Go in motion. Receive the pitch or handoff depending on the type of backfield action. Sprint wide and cut on the blocks of the playside halfback and fullback.

Quarterback—Reverse pivot and pitch the ball to the halfback. After the pitch lead the ballcarrier and become an extra blocker. As an alternate backfield action, open pivot and hand the ball to the halfback. Continue to the backside, faking a bootleg.

BOOTLEG BY THE QUARTERBACK

When running the Power Sweep one of the backfield actions features the quarterback handing the ball off to the halfback and then faking a bootleg to the backside. In diagram 7-13 the quarterback keeps the ball.

Both of the guards pull opposite the backfield flow and act as a blocking escort for the quarterback. Two blocks are critical: First, the playside tackle must fire out with his head in the middle of the defender, work the helmet past the defender's outside hip and hook him to the inside. Second, the playside guard must overthrow on the defensive end. The split end blocks the inside safety, while the backside guard will attack the defensive halfback. The diagram shows the play being run into the split end side of a Double Slot formation.

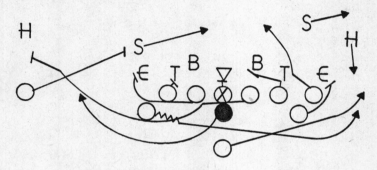

Diagram 7-13

HALFBACK REVERSE OFF THE POWER SWEEP

A misdirection play off the Power Sweep action is shown in diagram 7-14. The motion halfback hands the ball off to the stationary halfback coming back inside across the offensive formation. The quarterback uses a hand-off technique and becomes a blocker as he fakes the bootleg action. The offensive guards direction step for the Power Sweep, they then pivot back and lead the reverse action.

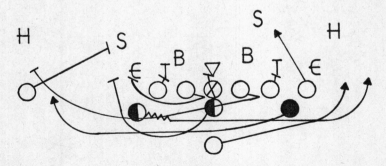

Diagram 7-14

BASIC TECHNIQUES FOR THE REVERSE

Playside end—Release shallow and block the inside safety. Look for the shallow linebacker vs. an 8-man front.

Playside tackle—Block the man in the gap, the man on, or the linebacker over.

Playside guard—Pull 2 steps to the backside. Pivot back and over- throw block the defensive end to the inside.

Center—Block the man on or backside.

Backside guard—Pull to the backside for two steps. Pivot back and pull shallow, kick out on the contain man.

Backside tackle—Block #2 defend.

Backside end—Release and block the middle 1/3.

Playside halfback—Go in motion and receive a hand-off from the quarterback. Hand the ball to the other halfback coming back to the inside across the formation.

Fullback—Fake a sweep to the backside.

Backside halfback—Pivot back to the inside. Receive the hand-off and sprint to the outside. Cut on the blocks of the quar- terback and playside guard.

Quarterback—Open pivot and hand the ball to the motion back. Carry out a bootleg action and lead the reverse play downfield.

The Reverse against an 8 man front is shown in diagram 7-15.

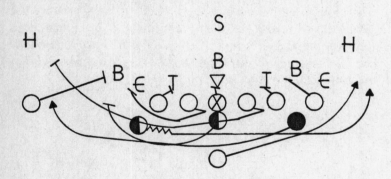

Diagram 7-15

KEY COACHING POINTS FOR THE REVERSE

1) Good misdirection techniques by the offensive guards.
2) Shallow release and screen block to the inside by the split end.

3) A good sweep fake by the playside halfback. The ball is handed off to the inside and this technique must be practiced.

4) The quarterback uses a hand-off technique and becomes a blocker after he fakes his bootleg action.

NAMING SUPPLEMENTARY
DOUBLE SLOT RUNNING PLAYS

1) End Around—No numbering application; a special play so it is called as "End Around." The play action type will have to be called in the huddle. Veer action, Fullback Option action, etc.

2) Tight End Sweep—Again a special play, so no application of the numbering system. Slant action must be specified when making the call in the huddle.

3) Power Sweep—To the right, "19 Power Sweep."
To the left, "41 Power Sweep."
The type of backfield action must be called in the huddle, either pitch or hand-off.

4) Bootleg—To the right, "29 Bootleg Power Sweep."
To the left, "21 Bootleg Power Sweep."

5) Halfback Reverse—To the right, "19 Power Sweep Reverse."
To the left, "41 Power Sweep Reverse."

8

Developing
Pass Play Calling
and Summary of
Secondary Coverages

RELEASE TECHNIQUES BY RECEIVERS

Receivers vary their splits according to the strategy described in Chapter 1. The receiver must drive as hard and low as possible when releasing from his 3-point stance. The hard driving technique must be executed for at least three steps. The technique must look the same no matter what the offensive play happens to be. This release consistency is essential in that the defense determines what the offensive play action is by reading certain receiver maneuvers. The defense tries to determine whether the play is a run or pass for its own reactions. There are two release types: First, the outside release; this is used primarily for quick outside pass patterns when the defensive secondary is back deep. The outside release is also effective when running the draw play. When using the outside release in a draw situation, it tends to draw the defenders to the outside away from the ball action and point of attack. Also, an outside release tends to back up the safety man which aids in giving the draw play more running room.

Second is the inside release. This is used primarily by an inside receiver (tight end or slot back) when there is a defender playing on his outside shoulder. The inside release is a key for the defense. They may design their strategy so that an inside receiver is expected to release to the inside and any other maneuver by the offensive player will be a specific run or pass key for the defenders. This depends on the overall strategy of the defense. Generally it is a good idea to change the release technique to keep the defense honest.

BASIC PASS PATTERNS FOR RECEIVERS

Pass routes for all receivers are numbered. Each pass pattern is assigned a specific number from 0 through 9. Individual techniques may differ slightly for each receiver depending on whether he is aligned outside as a split end or inside as a tight end or halfback. The list and description of each route is as follows:

"0"—*Slide*—Use an outside release technique. Work straight to the outside at a 30-degree angle from the line of scrimmage. At a distance of 4 yards from the sideline, drive hard upfield and run a streak. This pattern is used primarily towards the wide side of the field or on "pick" type patterns with the playside halfback. This technique is illustrated in diagram 8-1 against a rotating corner secondary.

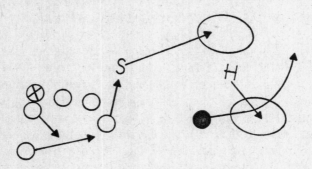

Diagram 8-1

"1"—*Hook*—Run the basic post technique. Take two steps into the post, then turn coming back towards the ball. The pattern is run primarily against man-to-man defenders. The pattern design does not work into the open seam on zone coverages. The Hook is shown in diagram 8-2.

"2"—*Square Out*—Drive off for a distance of 5-7 yards. Plant the inside foot and drive hard into the sideline. Work back towards the line of scrimmage at a slight angle. The pattern can be run by an outside or inside receiver. The square out is illustrated in diagram 8-3.

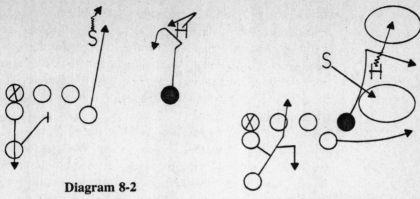

Diagram 8-2

Diagram 8-3

"3"—*Quick Look In*—Drive off for three steps. Get the defender to back up. Break to the inside at a 45-degree angle. Approximately 7/8 speed is used once the cut is made. Timing is important, as it is a difficult pass for the quarterback to throw. It is a good pattern against a defensive back that plays a deep cushion on the split receiver. The pattern is also effective to a tight end if the linebackers are involved in stunts. The Quick Look In is illustrated in diagrams 8-4A and 8-4B. In 8-4A the tight end runs the pattern against a stunting 4-3 middle linebacker. In 8-4B a split receiver runs the pattern vs. a cushioning inside safety.

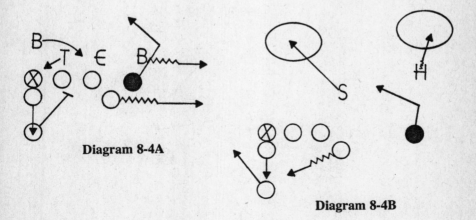

Diagram 8-4A

Diagram 8-4B

"4"—*Curl*—Run the post break for three steps. Plant and work back towards the line of scrimmage. Look for the lane between the drops of the linebackers in the "underneath" coverage. Work for that lane. Watch the coverage and quarterback. This pattern takes a great deal of practice but it is quite effective vs. zone coverages. Diagram 8-5 shows the curl pattern technique.

"5"—*Post*—Drive downfield for 5-8 yards. Fake slightly to the outside. Break toward the goal posts. Work across the field and turn up splitting the seam on zone coverage. By turning upfield, it is easier for the quarterback to throw in this direction, than have to throw the ball across the field. Diagram 8-6 shows the post being run at a secondary that "inverts" on flow.

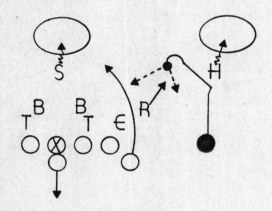

Diagram 8-5

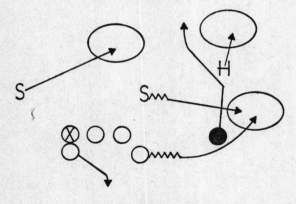

Diagram 8-6

"6"—*Flag*—Make a good fake of the quick look in. This causes the defense to think the pattern is the quick look in and to rotate up fast to cover. This allows the pass receiver to break behind the defender. Plant the inside foot and drive back to the outside for the flag at the corner of the goal line. The flag may also be run off the post pattern technique if more depth is desired. The flag is illustrated in diagram 8-7 off the post action.

"7"—*Take Off*—Execute the basic square out technique. Take three steps into the cut of the square out pattern. Plant the outside foot and sprint straight downfield. A good fake on the square out pattern will draw the corner defender to play that technique. Should the receiver face a corner force rotation, then it is important to stay 4 yards from the sideline and away from the rotating inside safety. The take off is illustrated in diagram 8-8 against man-to-man coverage.

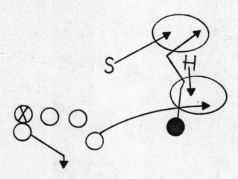

Diagram 8-7

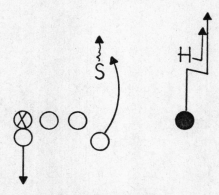

Diagram 8-8

"8"—*Streak*—This pattern primarily requires speed. Drive and run downfield as quickly as possible. Against a zone, read the rotation and know the open seams. Slow up slightly in these areas so the quarterback can deliver the ball. Against a man-to-man pull your head up slightly to get the defender thinking that a cut is going to be made. Hopefully the defender will hesitate a second. The streak pattern by a tight end is shown in diagram 8-9.

"9"—*Flat*—This pattern is for an inside receiver. Release inside or outside the defensive end, depending on how he aligns. Work for a varying depth of 3 to 4 yards. Drive downfield at a position 4 yards from the sideline. Diagram 8-10 shows the flat technique.

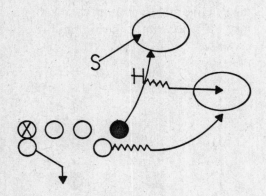

Diagram 8-9

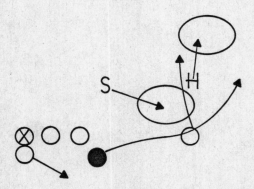

Diagram 8-10

NAMING THE PASS ACTIONS AND PATTERNS

The play action in the backfield may vary in different situations. Generally the type of backfield movements are named directly by the quarterback in the huddle. All play action passes are designated directly. For example, Veer action, Buck action, Slant action. Each one of these phrases names a specific action that is executed initially before the ball is delivered. All pass actions that involve no play fakes are also named directly. For example, Sprint Out, Rollout, and Dropback. Direction for a given backfield maneuver is named by using the words right or left. A sprint right pass would name the direction and specific backfield action for the play. The call also tells the offense to which side of the offensive formation the primary pass patterns will be run.

Pass patterns for specific recievers are designated using a 2 digit number. The first digit specifies the pass route to be run by the widest receiver. The second number designates the pass pattern to be run by the next receiver to the inside. Three man pass patterns can be included by adding a third digit to the call. Diagram 8-11 shows how the system will work for a 2-man pattern. The play is named as "Veer Right Action 49." The digit "4" has the split receiver running a Curl pattern, while the playside halfback releases on a flat route. An example of a 3-man pattern is illustrated in diagram 8-12. The huddle call would be made as "Sprint Right 628 Motion." The split end runs a flag off the post action. Because of the use of "motion" the second receiver to the inside now becomes the backside halfback; he runs a square out. The playside halfback is the third man to the inside and is assigned a pattern by the third digit in the play call; he runs a streak to occupy the middle safety. Numerous pass patterns and combinations can be incorporated once this calling system has been adapted.

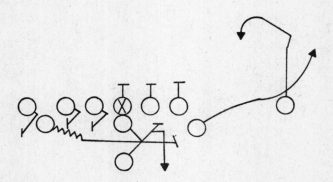

Diagram 8-11

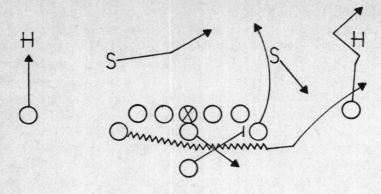

Diagram 8-12

SURVEY OF DEFENSIVE SECONDARY COVERAGES
AGAINST THE DOUBLE SLOT

The following is a breakdown as to how the various defensive strategies of the secondary react and adjust coverages against the Double Slot formations.

ZONE COVERAGES

3 Deep

The 3 deep defenses use two halfbacks and a middle safety. (Diagram 8-13.) Wide receivers should take maximum splits to isolate the halfbacks from support by the middle safety. Three deep secondaries use basically three coverage techniques against the Double Slot.

First, against a tight end, corner rotation can be used. In this situa-

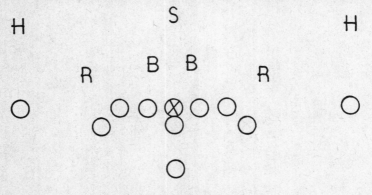

Diagram 8-13

tion the defensive halfback to the called coverage side rolls to cover the flat on dropback play action or on sprint or rollout to the coverage side. Should ball action develop away from the call, then the secondary defenders will play a "locked in" 3-deep zone, each covering the deep 1/3 of the field. Diagram 8-14 shows Sprint Out action to the coverage side. The halfback levels in the flat, the safety rolls to the deep outside 1/3, and the backside defensive halfback plays the backside 2/3 of the field. Halfback rotation towards a split end is shown in diagram 8-15. Because of the split end's position from the ball, the safetyman has a great distance to cover when the corner back (halfback) rotates to the flat. With this coverage the split end has a great deal of room to operate in the deep outside area. Limits of the 3 deep force the use of linebackers to drop into the shallow areas "underneath" the deep defenders.

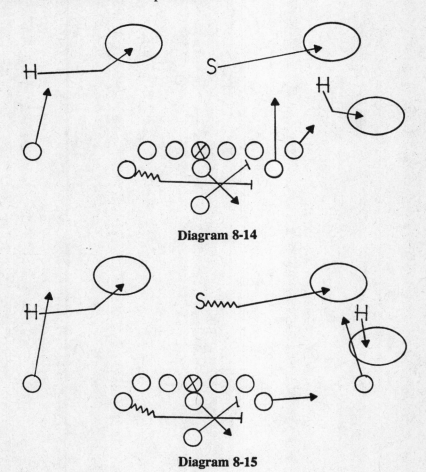

Diagram 8-14

Diagram 8-15

Second, the 3 deep may rotate to the weak side as a change up call. This rotation may take place to a tight end if motion goes away or to a split end, also when motion is directed away. The rotation call is in effect if the ball action is towards the weak side or dropback. A linebacker must cover the flat away from the call. Weakside rotation is illustrated in diagram 8-16. Should the offense sprint or play action to the strong side, then the secondary will "check off" and rotate this way or play a "locked in" 3-deep zone.

Third, the secondary may play a "locked in" 3 deep with outside linebackers responsible for flat coverage on ball action keys. This coverage technique is illustrated in diagram 8-17.

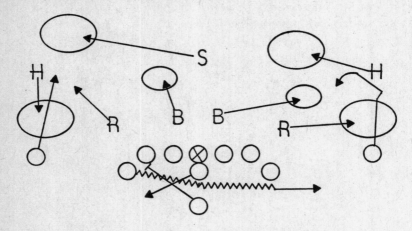

Diagram 8-16

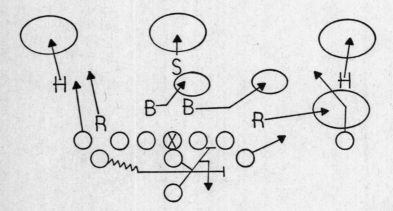

Diagram 8-17

4 Deep

Individual coverage designs from the 4 deep secondary are numerous. Generally they fall into two categories with zone coverage. One is a corner force technique where the defensive halfback rotates to the flat on ball action, formation strength, or dropback technique. Should the offense show a different key, then the secondary may re-rotate back away from the predetermined call. Diagram 8-18 shows the corner force coverage into a tight end side of an offensive formation. Diagram 8-18 also shows ball action and motion being directed towards a tight end. Each inside safety rotates to the deep outside 1/3 and to the deep middle 1/3 as shown in the diagrams.

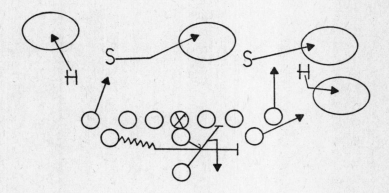

Diagram 8-18

Safety force rotation is shown in diagram 8-19. This coverage is most effective against a split end formation. It may be a predetermined call into strength, ball action, dropback or motion. The defense will re-rotate automatically should one of these keys not develop. As a basic technique, one of the inside safeties runs into the flat on a specific key. Safety force rotation is also shown in diagram 8-20 towards a tight end alignment.

Both of these calls may be used to the weak side of an offensive formation. This may be away from a tight end or away from motion. Diagram 8-21 shows safety force rotation to the weak side (away from a tight end and away from motion) against dropback pass action by the quarterback. Backside defenders show man-to-man techniques to their side.

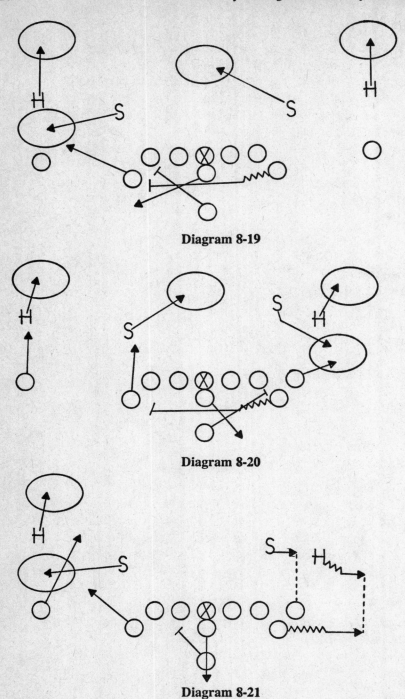

Diagram 8-19

Diagram 8-20

Diagram 8-21

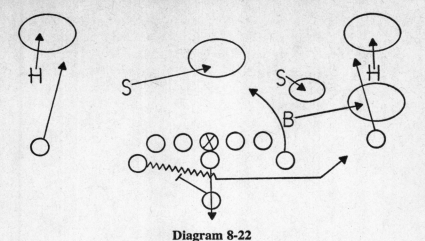

Diagram 8-22

A linebacker may also be used in 4-deep rotation coverage. In diagram 8-22, the outside linebacker in a 4-3 defense rotates to the outside flat. The defensive halfback drops to the deep outside 1/3, while the inside safety to the rotation call plays the hook zone which was the original coverage assignment for the outside linebacker.

MAN-TO-MAN COVERAGES

3 Deep

Each defender is assigned a potential offensive receiver whom he must cover all over the field. The defensive back should align so that he will initially take away the most effective pass cut by the receiver. Diagram 8-23 shows coverage man-to-man from the 3 deep. The two

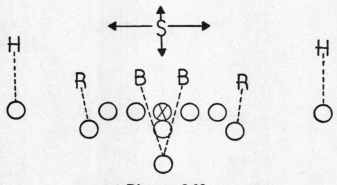

Diagram 8-23

halfbacks take the split receivers. Each outside linebacker is assigned to cover a halfback, while the safety is "free" to play the ball. Actually the safety may help out on the coverage of an outstanding pass receiver. The only time that a change in man-to-man techniques will occur is when the offense runs any sort of crossing patterns. Here the deep defenders call "switch" and immediately exchange coverage responsibilities when the receivers make their breaks. This technique is illustrated in diagram 8-24.

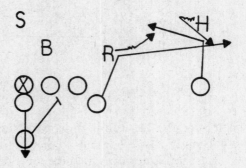

Diagram 8-24

4 Deep

Four deep man-to-man coverage vs. the Double Slot is shown in diagram 8-25. Basically the philosophy of the 3 deep is carried over. The defenders align to play the best pass cut of the receiver. "Switch" calls are worked against crossing patterns.

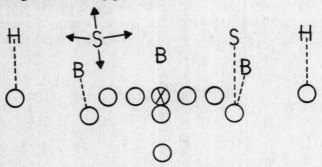

Diagram 8-25

COMBINATIONS

Both 3-deep and 4-deep secondaries can use combination coverages against the Double Slot. These are categorized generally as coverages that utilize both man-to-man and zone. In diagram 8-26 a 3-deep combination pattern is shown. In this situation the secondary executes rotation towards motion, ball action or formation strength. The backside defensive halfback covers the backside receiver man-to-man. Linebackers are used to cover the "underneath" areas. Diagram 8-27 shows combination zone coverage to the tight end side, while the backside defensive halfback plays man-to-man. The remaining safety becomes free to play the ball or help on some sort of double coverage.

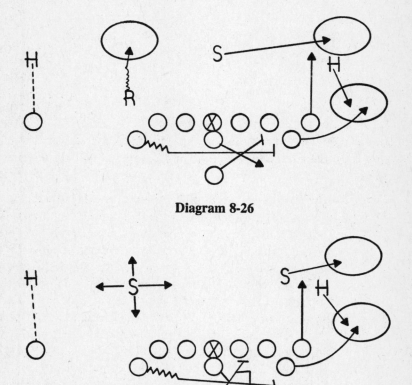

Diagram 8-26

Diagram 8-27

MAN-TO-MAN COMBINATIONS 4 DEEP

This coverage is shown in diagram 8-28. Each defender has a specific key. The halfbacks will cover the split receivers man-to-man. Each inside safety will key the tight end (or specific halfback in the direc-

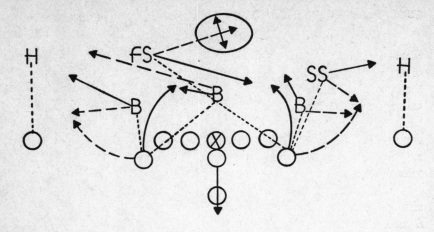

Diagram 8-28

tion of the call). The outside linebackers also have specific keys that are primarily from the backfield. Assignments and techniques for the man to man combination coverages are as follows (based on a 4-3 Pro defense).

Defensive halfbacks—Play man-to-man on the widest receiver.

Strong Safety—Align to the side of the call and key the first inside receiver. If the receiver releases inside, help the defensive halfback with the wide man. When helping the defensive halfback, take away any inside routes by the wide receiver. Should the key use an outside release, play him on any inside cuts that he might make.

Free Safety—Key the tight end to the side of the call. Cover the tight end (or slot back) on any inside cuts. If the key makes a cut to the outside, "zone" the middle playing the ball.

Middle Linebacker—Key the halfback away from the call (may be a tight end away from a call). Play the receiver on any inside cuts. If the receiver releases to the outside, work wide, taking away the angle on the quick slant pass to the split receiver.

Outside Linebackers—If on the call side, key the near halfback. Cover him man-to-man all the way. If to the side away from the call, key the near halfback and cover him on the out cut. If the halfback releases to the inside, get into the throwing lane for the out cut of the split receiver.

SECONDARY ADJUSTMENTS TO MOTION

Defensive secondaries will tend to zone with pre-rotation on any motion action. A predetermined zone may be rotated to on the snap as a change up. Against "fly" motion the secondary will play a pre-rotation technique in that it will declare its coverage as the motion begins. The secondary may flow quickly into its coverage as the ball is snapped. "Fly" motion is used on play action passes off the Veer series. In covering and adjusting to "fly" with a man-to-man concept, the secondary uses a "free" safety, with the remaining members "locked on" their individual keys.

Should the defense face "jet" motion, it may pre-rotate to the "jet" side only or lock into some form of man-to-man coverage. Usually an 8-man front (5-3 and 4-4 defenses) will adjust to "jet" by dropping off an outside linebacker. Diagrams 8-29, 8-30 and 8-31 illustrate various situations of secondary coverages when facing "fly" and "jet" motion. Dia-

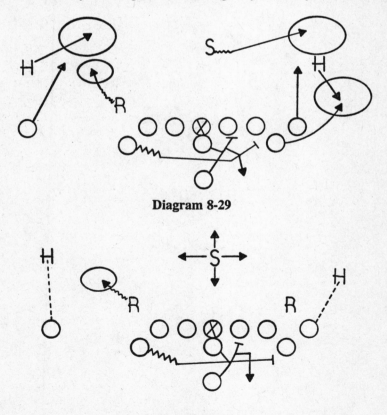

Diagram 8-29

Diagram 8-30

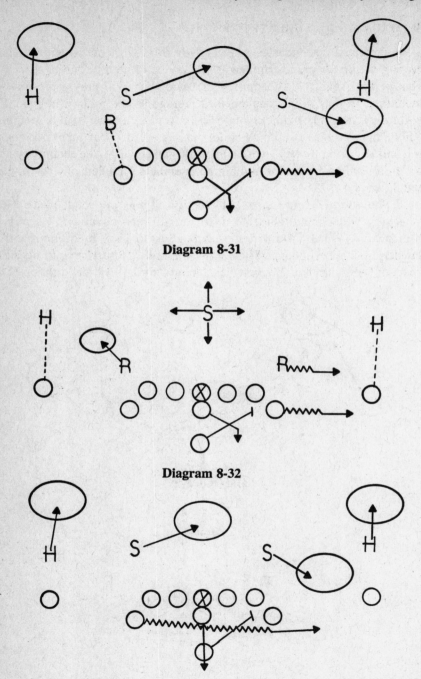

Diagram 8-31

Diagram 8-32

Diagram 8-33

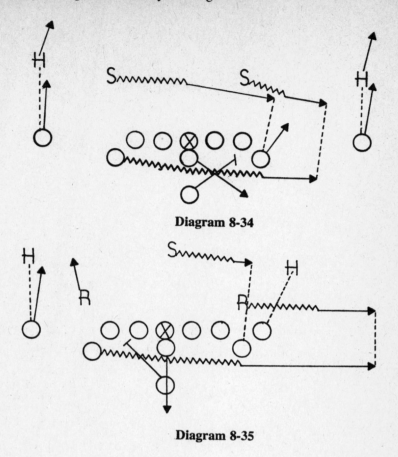

Diagram 8-34

Diagram 8-35

gram 8-32 shows an 8-man front with a linebacker covering the "jet" man while the halfbacks play man-to-man with a free safety.

Against "motion" a number of adjustments can be utilized. Generally "motion" requires the most radical adjustment within the secondary. "Motion" is an excellent means to aid the offense in determining the various secondary strategies when developing the passing attack. Diagrams 8-33, 8-34, and 8-35 show various adjustments and schemes vs. "motion." In 8-33 a 4-deep rotating zone compensates by pre-rotating the inside safety to the flat once the motioning halfback gets outside the position of the offensive tackle. Diagram 8-34 illustrates man-to-man adjustments; in this situation the two inside safeties work together mirroring the movements of the halfback. A compensation by a 3-deep secondary is shown in diagram 8-35. Here the outside linebacker drops off in man-to-man coverage on the halfback as the motion moves outside.

9

Establishing the Double Slot Pass Actions

BASIC PASS ACTIONS

In the Double Slot attack the following backfield actions will be used to establish the various launch points for the passing game. Three basic maneuvers will be used with slight modification of each technique in accordance with the desired launch point, pass patterns of receivers, and various coverages developed by the defensive secondary.

ROLLOUT

First in the series of backfield actions is the rollout. Here the quarterback reverse pivots and sprints to the launch point. Generally the quarterback can deliver the ball to receivers while on the run, providing that the pass patterns are outside cuts. For any pattern that is run to the inside, the quarterback must plant and set up before delivering the ball. The quarterback can deliver the ball on the run to outside patterns because the momentum of his body is moving in this direction and the throwing of the ball is a natural extension of this movement.

If the quarterback throws the ball to inside patterns while on the run, it is a most difficult technique. Here the quarterback is forced to throw the ball across his body, opposite the direction in which he is moving. A lot of force and throwing accuracy is lost. As a result the quarterback must pull up by planting the lead foot and deliver the ball from the set position. Diagram 9-1A shows the "out" passing relationship with the quarterback, while diagram 9-1B shows the quarterback setting up to deliver the inside pass routes. This latter action is often referred to as a semi-roll technique. Individual techniques for the quarterback are as follows:

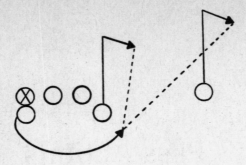

Diagram 9-1A

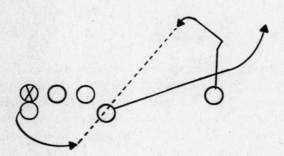

Diagram 9-1B

1) Carry most of the weight on the foot to the side in which the roll-out technique will take place. If rolling to the right, push off hard on the right foot and bring the left foot back around, planting it in the desired direction.

2) The ball is brought to the belt buckle. As the second step is taken, the quarterback must snap his head around and look for the called pattern.

3) The ball should be ready for delivery on the third step. Overall the play action should be on an angle of 45 degrees from the line of scrimmage. The quarterback should gain depth to approximately 6 yards behind the playside offensive tackle.

4) *Semi-Roll* technique. This is the set-up technique used when throwing inside patterns. All the fundamental rollout techniques are the same except that the quarterback will now set up at a

depth of 6 to 7 yards behind the offensive tackle, then deliver the ball.

SPRINT OUT

The sprint technique is a direct open pivot by the quarterback, attacking immediately outside the position of the tight end. All outside patterns can be thrown while on the run. Each inside pattern requires the quarterback to set up behind the outside leg of the offensive tackle before throwing the ball. The same principles as in the rollout are carried over to the sprint out action. The sprint out places more pressure on the defensive corner, with not only the various pass routes, but also the threat of the quarterback running with the ball. Key coaching points for the sprint out technique are as follows:

1) Pivot off the opposite foot and "throw out" the direction foot. As the initial step is taken the ball is brought up to the passing shoulder while simultaneously focusing the eyes on the pass patterns and secondary keys.
2) As the second step is planted the ball must be ready for delivery.
3) It should take approximately five steps for the quarterback to reach his initial point which is 4 to 6 yards behind the position of the tight end.
4) Upon reaching his position the quarterback should turn his shoulders upfield parallel to the line of scrimmage. This facilitates the passing of the ball upfield. (*Note:* When sprinting to the left and the quarterback is right handed, he requires an extra step to get his shoulders turned around.)
5) The depth factor is critical. The most common mistake is for the quarterback to get too much depth which tends to cause a disruption in the timing of the pass pattern. The quarterback should work a somewhat rounded course, getting no deeper than 4 to 6 yards.
6) *Semi-Sprint technique*. This is the set-up technique off the sprint action. The quarterback pulls up behind the outside leg of the playside tackle. From here delivery of the ball can be directed to the inside, deep outside, or throwback across the field. The quarterback will set up on the fifth or sixth step, read the secondary and linebacker coverages.

Diagrams 9-2A and 9-2B illustrate the sprint out and semi-sprint out techniques along with the complementary passing trees.

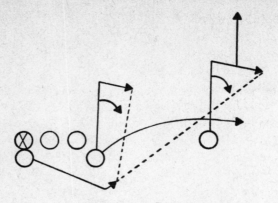

Diagram 9-2A

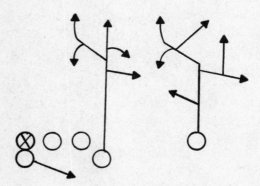

Diagram 9-2B

DROPBACK

As a third backfield action the dropback is utilized. Two basic types are used, the deep drop and quick drop. The deep drop features a body pivot with the quarterback sprinting back directly to a depth of 8 to 9 yards. The quick dropback features a back pedal technique with the quarterback reading his keys and delivering the ball very quickly as he retreats from the line of scrimmage.

Dropback Techniques

1) Push off the left foot and get as deep as possible with the right foot.
2) Turn the shoulders so that they are perpendicular to the line of scrimmage and parallel to the sideline. The right foot must be

planted directly behind the left so that the quarterback gets back in a straight line.

3) The second step is a cross over by the left foot. This step again must be as deep as possible.

4) The ball is brought up on the third step as the quarterback looks downfield for the read keys. The third step is directly in line with the second step. This sequence of steps is repeated to a depth of 7 to 8 yards.

Back Pedal Technique

1) On the snap the quarterback runs backwards. As he moves back the ball is brought up to chest level and the shoulders are kept parallel to the line of scrimmage.

2) This technique is used primarily in the quick dropback passing attack. It allows a quick reading of the defense and a quick delivery of the ball should a stunt occur.

Dropback launch points are illustrated in diagrams 9-3A and 9-3B.

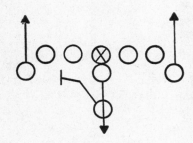

Diagram 9-3A

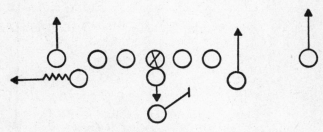

Diagram 9-3B

BLOCKING ASSIGNMENTS AND TECHNIQUES

Because the pass game is divided into three basic phases, different blocking patterns must be developed to effectively protect the various launch points. These launch points will be determined by the type of ball action employed in the pass play. Each blocking scheme is broken down into specific assignments for playside linemen and backside linemen. The backs, especially the fullback, have very important roles in the overall protection scheme. It is important that they understand the assignments of the offensive line and various defensive structures so that effective coordination can be developed.

SPRINT AND ROLLOUT PROTECTION ASSIGNMENTS

The following is a breakdown of the blocking schemes used in the sprint and rollout pass actions. Unless the quarterback is attempting to throw inside pass patterns, he will be sprinting outside the end defender. The defensive end is assigned to the fullback. On sprint out (or rollout) action where the quarterback is throwing outside pass patterns, it is desirable that the fullback hook the defensive end to the inside. This allows the quarterback to get outside the contain with a run or pass option. On "inside" pass routes (semi-sprint techniques), the fullback drives the end defender to the outside because the quarterback sets up before delivering the ball. Sprint and rollout assignments and techniques are as follows:

Playside tackle—Block the defender head on or to the outside. The blocker must aim low and scramble block the defender (use all fours) never allowing any penetration. On passes where the quarterback sets up, the tackle must fire out and stay as square as possible to the defender. By staying square the blocker makes himself as big as geometrically possible in relation to the launch point.

Playside guard—Block the first defender from the center out. If there is a man on the guard, scramble block as for the offensive tackle. Should there be a linebacker over the guard as in the 5-2 defense, the guard will fire out with the inside foot and key the linebacker wherever he goes. If the linebacker drops into coverage, the guard helps the center and playside tackle with their blocks. Helping the playside tackle is illustrated in diagram 9-4A. In diagram 9-4B the guard picks the stunting linebacker, as the defender loops around the defensive tackle. The guard must

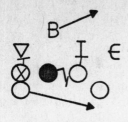

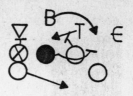

Diagram 9-4B

Diagram 9-4A

work to get as square as possible when picking up the stunt.

Center—Scramble block the man on. If uncovered, key the middle linebacker. Set up and help out if the linebacker drops into coverage. Pick him up if he blitzes. Diagram 9-5 shows a common stunt from the 4-3. When setting up, the center uses a wide foot base, the hips bent, head up and back straight. Keep the feet moving so that an adjustment to defensive seepage and stunts can be made.

Diagram 9-5

Backside guard—Hinge technique.
Backside tackle—Hinge technique.

HINGE TECHNIQUE (INDIVIDUAL)

Hinge blocking is designed to create a wall concept to the backside. Each lineman sets up to the inside and tries to stay as large as possible between the defensive pass rusher and the launch point. The individual lineman must be effectively coached in the following techniques.

1) Know the launch point from where the pass will be thrown.
2) Push off the up foot and step back to the inside. If uncovered get off the line at least 4 feet. This puts the offensive player in a position to pick up stunting defenders coming into his area. If covered work for an inside-out position, but not as deep.

3) Keep the inside foot forward and planted. Set low and keep the back flat. Stay crouched with a good bend in the knees. Stay low and agile.

4) Turn the tail to the launch point. Force the defender to charge through the long axis (length) of your body. Stay head up and square (as big as geometrically possible). Don't allow the defender the inside route.

5) Deliver the blow when the defender is almost against you; don't overcommit. Keep the head up and recoil as soon as the defender has been hit. "Hit low then get low."

6) When losing the defender, use a bump-and-throw technique. Aim for the defender's far hip and get the head across.

7) Cover the pass downfield after it is thrown.

DROPBACK PROTECTION

Two basic schemes are used in the dropback or "cup" protection. Each one of these blocking schemes is determined by the number of receivers to a given side. For example when releasing 3 receivers on one side, the blocking must be adjusted to compensate and seal the playside. For the guard and tackle, their assignments remain unchanged; they block the first and second defenders at the line of scrimmage. All adjustments are made by the offensive center. Each of the blocking schemes is outlined as follows:

Dropback Protection for 2-Man Pass Patterns

Guards—Block the first defender on the line of scrimmage from the center.

Tackles—Block the second defender from the center on the line of scrimmage.

Center—Block the defender over. Check the linebacker to the backside. Help to the playside.

Dropback Protection for 3-Man Pass Patterns

Guards—Block #1 on the line of scrimmage.

Tackles—Block #2 on the line of scrimmage.

Center—Block the defender over. Check the first linebacker to the playside. Help out backside.

Individual Dropback Protection Techniques

Techniques vary in dropback or "cup" protection. A combination of the hit and ride technique is used in the Double Slot offense. In this blocking skill, the ride phase controls the defender and the offensive blocker is likely to be in a less vulnerable position than if he used the hit and recoil technique. The Double Slot formation, releasing so many receivers, requires that the offensive blocker buy as much time as possible for the quarterback. Actually the geometry of the formation is not the best for the dropback passing game.

When describing this blocking technique it is essential that the offensive line understand the various rush lanes that may be taken by the defense. Defenses constantly undergo changes and offensive linemen must practice against different rush types and angles.

On the snap the offensive lineman will jab step to the inside to establish an inside-out approach to the rusher. In the Double Slot, the offensive blockers should drive the defenders to the outside as much as possible, allowing the quarterback time to operate as well and provide him with sufficient vision to read the secondary coverages. Remaining techniques are the same as outlined for individual hinge blocking. Instead of hitting and recoiling, the offensive blocker must lock on to the defender and ride him to the outside as far away from the launch point as possible. It is also important that the offensive blocker slide step initially to the inside and when making contact be as square as possible from an inside-out position. Diagrams 9-6 and 9-7 illustrate the dropback blocking assignments for 2-man patterns, while diagram 9-8 shows the protection scheme in a 3-man pattern situation.

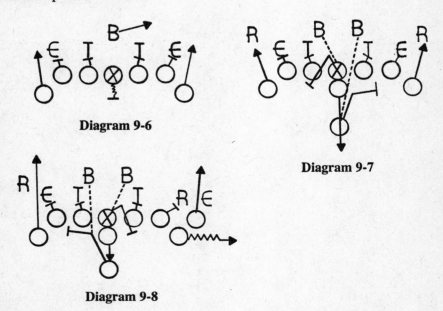

Diagram 9-6

Diagram 9-7

Diagram 9-8

BACKFIELD BLOCKING
ASSIGNMENTS AND TECHNIQUES

Sprint and Rollout

In all sprint and rollout pass actions the fullback will lead block to the playside. His assignment is to block the end defender on the line of scrimmage. Two techniques will be used by the fullback. Each technique will depend upon the type of action used by the quarterback as well as the styles of pass patterns to be thrown. Should the pass play be a sprint out with the receivers executing out routes, then the fullback will hook the defensive end to the inside. This allows the quarterback to not only get outside the defensive contain but also threaten the defensive corner with the run or pass. On inside pass patterns where the quarterback pulls up before throwing, the fullback will drive block the defensive end to the outside. This provides the passer with a pocket effect from which to throw the ball. Each situation is illustrated in diagrams 9-9 and 9-10.

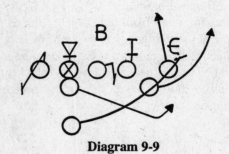

Diagram 9-9

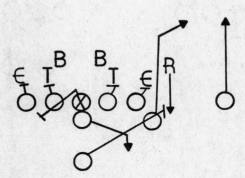

Diagram 9-10

INDIVIDUAL TECHNIQUES FOR THE FULLBACK

1) For the hook block, the fullback aims for the outside hip of the end defender. On contact the fullback must sink his hip into the defensive end and scramble on all fours, taking the defender upfield.

2) For the lead block, the fullback attacks the defender on the same angle as the hook block. On contact the blocker drives the helmet past the inside hip of the defender and rides him to the outside. As the defensive end is blocked, the fullback must stay as square as possible between the defender and the quarterback.

The backside halfback may use a number of techniques. These will vary depending upon the motion type that is used in the play. He may use "fly" motion and help the fullback seal the defensive end to the inside. This scheme is illustrated in diagram 9-11. Also using "fly" the halfback may pivot to the backside and help against the rush. This is shown in diagram 9-12. The halfback may be required to stay in and block on the

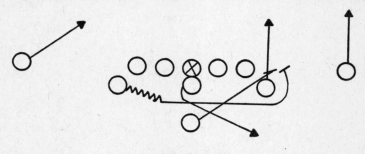

Diagram 9-11

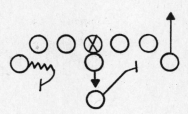

Diagram 9-12

backside when a great deal of pressure is being encountered. The blocking call is made in the huddle using the word "Max." Primarily "Max" is used when the quarterback is sprinting in the direction of "jet" motion.

"Max" is shown in diagram 9-13. On 3-man pass patterns the backside halfback usually is involved in the play as a result of "motion." Should the fullback be designated as a third receiver and release into the pattern, then the halfback will assume his blocking assignment, depending upon the type of action used by the quarterback. Diagram 9-14 shows the fullback running a Flat pattern while the halfback (backside) now attacks the defensive end.

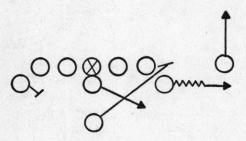

Diagram 9-13

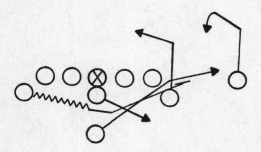

Diagram 9-14

BACKFIELD ASSIGNMENTS
FOR DROPBACK PROTECTION

Fullback

1) On any 3-man pass play, unless the fullback is the third receiver, he will block to the backside away from the call of the 3-man route. The fullback's assignment is to first check for a blitz by the first inside linebacker; he then helps out with the rush with the offensive linemen. In diagram 9-15, the fullback blocks the shooting linebacker in a 5-2 defense, while in diagram 9-16 he watches the linebacker drop into the pass coverage, so he pivots outside helping the guard with his block.

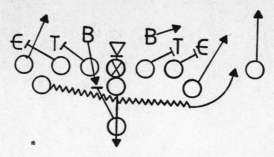

Diagram 9-15

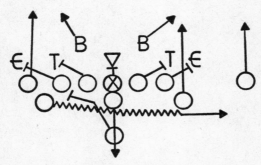

Diagram 9-16

2) On any 2-man pass patterns, the fullback will direct his block to the playside. This complements the block of the offensive center who has the backside linebacker as his responsibility. As he sets to the playside, the fullback checks for the rush of the inside linebacker. If the backer drops into coverage, then the fullback slides to the outside and helps the guard and tackle with their blocks on the pattern side. This technique is illustrated in diagram 9-16. Should the word "cup" be called in the huddle, the fullback will automatically block to the backside no matter what type of pass pattern has been designated. "Cup" designates that the backside halfback will use "fly" motion and block to the playside on 2-man pass patterns.

ASSIGNMENTS AND TECHNIQUES FOR HALFBACKS

There are numerous possibilities and combinations for the backside halfback. A great deal will depend on the type of motion called and the number of receivers in the designated pattern. If "jet" motion is used, then the halfback will stay in and block or may be given a safety valve

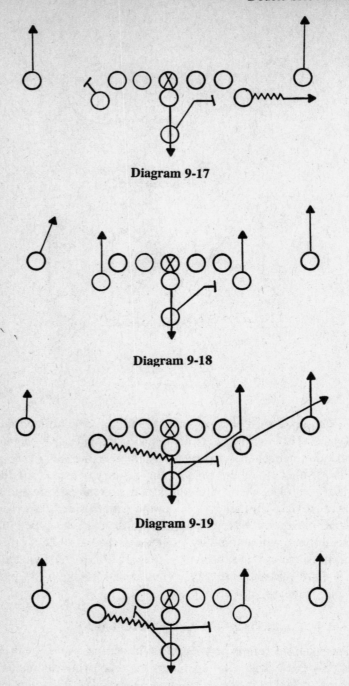

Diagram 9-17

Diagram 9-18

Diagram 9-19

Diagram 9-20

route. Diagram 9-17 shows the halfback blocking while in 9-18 he releases into the pattern. "Fly" motion will have the halfback blocking to
the playside if the pattern is 3-man and involves the fullback. He may also
be blocking to the playside if "fly" is called and also "cup" is specified
in the huddle. On normal 2-man patterns, the halfback will just pivot back
and block backside if involved with "fly" motion.

If "motion" is used, then chances are quite good that the halfback
will be involved in the primary pass pattern. "Motion" is used in 3-man
patterns that include the backside halfback. Diagram 9-19 shows the
halfback blocking to the playside from "fly" motion with the fullback releasing as the third man into the pass pattern. "Cup" blocking with "fly"
motion is illustrated in diagram 9-20.

TEAM PROTECTION TECHNIQUES

The following diagrams show applications of the various protection
blocking schemes. In diagram 9-21 sprint protection is shown against a
stunting 5-2 defense. "Jet" motion with a "Max" call on the backside is
featured.

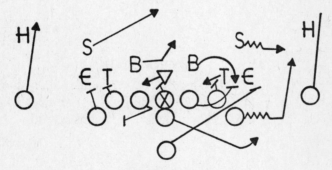

Diagram 9-21

Diagram 9-22 shows sprint protection with "fly" motion and a
3-man pattern with the fullback releasing into the playside flat. Because
of the "fly" motion, the backside halfback attacks the defensive end from
inside-out. The play action by the quarterback is semi-sprint.

A 2-man pattern with "jet" motion is the situation depicted in diagram 9-23. The defense is a 5-2 with both inside linebackers as part of the
rush. The fullback sets up and blocks the inside linebacker to the
playside. Against the 5-2 defense, backside guards must check first for
the rush of the linebacker before helping in other areas. This means that

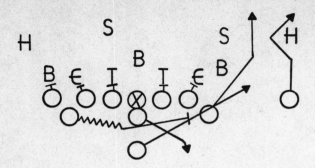

Diagram 9-22

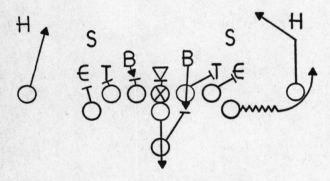

Diagram 9-23

the backside offensive tackle must block the defender aligned on him. In the diagram the backside guard picks up the shooting linebacker, while the backside halfback stays in and blocks the defensive end.

10

Coaching the Double Slot
Sprint Out Pass Game

A complete and effective sprint out pass game can be developed using the Double Slot formation. Various defensive coverages can be controlled and the resulting vacated areas of the field attacked. Primary pass route areas in the sprint out pass game are shown in diagram 10-1, and include the deep outside, middle outside, (deep flat), flat, curl and hook zones.

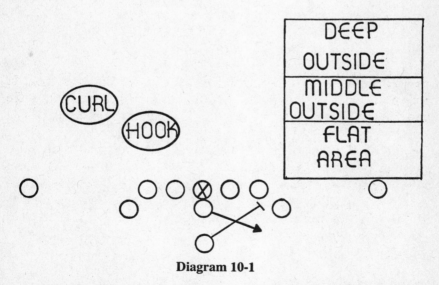

Diagram 10-1

Basic backfield action features the quarterback moving to the outside of the formation, while the fullback directs his block at the defensive end. On full sprint action the fullback must hook block the end defender to the inside, which pressures the defensive corner with a run or pass threat from the quarterback. When throwing to receivers running inside routes, the quarterback still moves to the outside but will pull up short, setting behind the outside leg of the playside tackle. He then throws the ball off planted feet, making the throw to the inside much easier. To establish this throwing "pocket," the fullback directs his block so that the end defender is driven to the outside. The angle of the block is from inside-out by the fullback.

Primarily 2-man patterns are run to the action side. Remaining receivers (a tight end and/or backside halfback) generally become part of the protection scheme. Basic "passing trees" for the split end and playside halfback are illustrated in diagram 10-2.

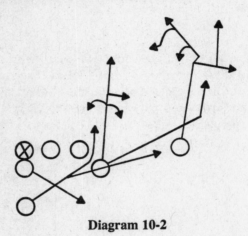

Diagram 10-2

ONE-MAN PATTERNS

In running single man pass patterns, the offense can establish maximum protection to the playside allowing the quarterback a great deal of time to throw the football. In addition to the block of the fullback, the playside halfback will also block on the defensive end. By sealing the defensive end (defensive contain) the corner is now open to the quarterback with a run-throw option. The primary receiver is the split end and he will run a number of different pass routes.

JET LEFT SPRINT RIGHT 2

Diagram 10-3 illustrates a typical one-man pattern with sprint out play action. Because only a single receiver is running the primary route, only one digit is called in the huddle to name the desired pass pattern. In

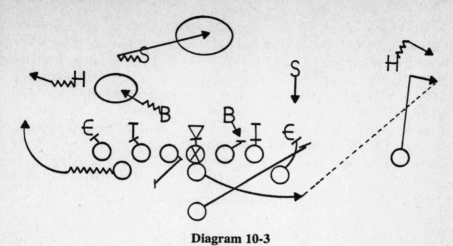

Diagram 10-3

this situation the split end is running a square out at 7 yards. On the backside the halfback moves in "jet" motion to the outside. To the playside both the fullback and halfback direct their blocks to seal the end defender to the inside. The quarterback can now get outside the contain and threaten the corner with a run or pass.

JET RIGHT SPRINT RIGHT 4

Another single receiver pattern is shown in diagram 10-4 from a tight end formation. The primary receiver is the playside halfback running

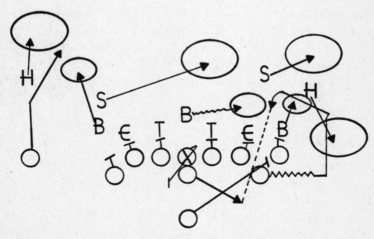

Diagram 10-4

a curl pattern off the "jet" motion. Both the fullback and tight end block the defensive end. Because of the inside design of the curl pattern, the blockers must drive the end defender to the outside, creating a launch pocket for the quarterback. As he moves to the outside, the quarterback pulls up at a depth of 6 yards and reads the "underneath" coverage. The key in the "underneath" coverage is the drop by the outside linebacker. The ball is delivered opposite his move. As the halfback runs his route, he should watch the angle of drop by the linebacker. The receiver must be ready to slide opposite the defender's move.

TWO-MAN PATTERNS

FLY RIGHT SPRINT RIGHT 49

Diagram 10-5 shows sprint action with a 2-man primary pattern, attacking a 5-2 defense. The defensive alignment has adjusted to the split end by moving into an "Eagle" look. The 4-deep secondary plays a "corner force" technique on sprint action. In this defensive coverage, the halfback to the action side revolves and levels in the flat, while the two safeties cover the outside and middle 1/3 areas as shown. Patterns for the primary receivers feature a curl by the split end that works the pattern opposite the drop of the "Eagle" linebacker. The playside halfback runs a flat route, working upfield into the deep outside 1/3. On the backside the tight end stays in and becomes part of the hinge protection being set up by the backside interior linemen. The backside halfback goes into "fly" motion and blocks along with the fullback on the defensive end to the playside. Both offensive blockers drive the defensive end to the outside. This establishes the throwing pocket for the quarterback, allowing him to set up and read the defensive reactions before throwing the ball. The primary receiver will be the split end working the curl route. As he sprints to the outside, the quarterback watches for the open lane to the curl pattern. Should the playside halfback be open early, then the quarterback will throw to him as the receiver makes his break upfield.

JET RIGHT SPRINT RIGHT 81

A second 2-man pattern is shown in diagram 10-6 against a 3-deep 4-4 defense. The secondary of the defense is rotating on ball action as its primary key. "Jet" motion to the playside loosens the defensive halfback to the outside flat. On the snap the safety revolves over to cover the deep outside 1/3. The key for the safety to move in this direction is the way that both the fullback and quarterback sprint to the outside. Off the "jet" mo-

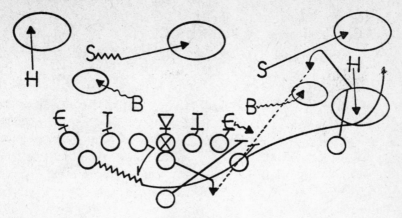

Diagram 10-5

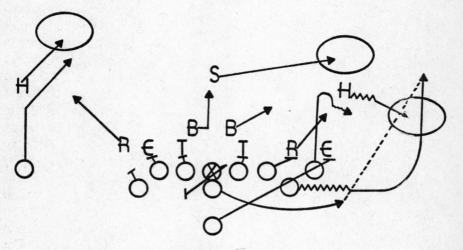

Diagram 10-6

tion, the playside halfback runs a streak down the sidelines. The tight end releases and runs a hook out at 8 yards. As the quarterback sprints to the outside, he looks for the halfback deep. The halfback should be open in the outside seam as the safetyman has so far to cover from the inside. The "underneath" coverage features one of the outside linebackers dropping off to get into the throwing lane for the out hook cut by the tight end. An inside linebacker plays the hook zone on the playside. "Max" blocking is used to the backside with the halfback staying in as part of the hinge blocking scheme. The split end runs a post pattern to occupy the zoning 2/3 defender. The playside halfback is the primary receiver, and if he is covered the quarterback should look to the tight end on the hook cut. Because of the zone techniques in the drops of the linebackers, there is a good chance that the tight end will be open in the seam.

JET RIGHT SPRINT RIGHT 85

"Jet" motion is again utilized in diagram 10-7 against the 4-3 defense. The inside safety adjusts to the motion man by using man-to-man coverage techniques. The defensive halfback covers the split end, also using man-to-man techniques. Zone coverage is played by the two secondary defenders to the backside. Primary patterns consist of the split end running a square in and the halfback a deep streak to the outside 1/3. When the split end makes his cut he must accelerate away from the defensive halfback and work into the open area. As control on the zone coverage to the backside, the split end releases and runs into the deep post seam. Playside protection must allow the quarterback to set up and look for the split end on the square in technique.

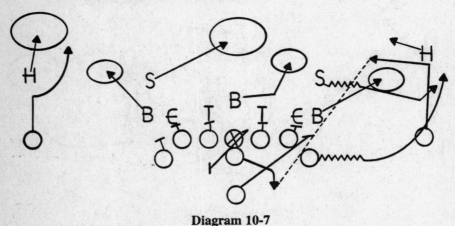

Diagram 10-7

THREE MAN PASS COMBINATIONS

On sprint action from the Double Slot, three potential receivers can be released into the playside pass patterns. The third receiver becomes the backside halfback using "motion" or the fullback sliding out into the flat off his sprint block action.

MOTION RIGHT SPRINT RIGHT 945

Diagram 10-8 illustrates "motion" by the backside halfback with a set of primary pass patterns designed to attack invert rotation from a 5-2

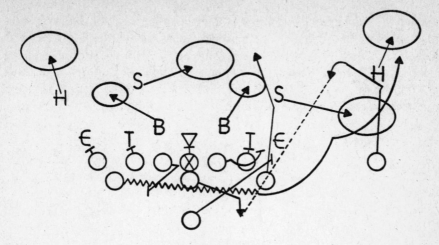

Diagram 10-8

defense. The split end runs a curl, working into the open seam between the dropping inside linebackers. The backside halfback comes off "motion" and runs an up pattern into the deep 1/3. The halfback to the playside keeps the backside safety busy by running a post route in the vacated middle 1/3 zone. The quarterback sprints and sets up to read the coverage. As a result the fullback directs his block to drive the end defender to the outside. The key for the quarterback is the action of the safety. Should the defender invert, the quarterback will throw to the split end on the curl. If the safety hangs or moves to the outside to cover the split man, then the quarterback will hit the "motion" back deep and to the outside.

FLY RIGHT SPRINT RIGHT 21 FULLBACK FLAT

.A rollout technique by the quarterback is featured in diagram 10-9. A 3-man pattern is also developed with the fullback sliding out into the flat. The backside halfback runs "fly" motion and now is responsible for blocking the defensive end to the playside. The backside halfback must hook and seal the defender to the inside, giving the corner to the quarterback. Primary patterns consist of the split end running an out cut, the playside halfback an out hook, and the fullback working into the flat. The backside tight end sets as if part of the hinge protection. If the defender on or outside him rushes, then the end will block the defender. Should the defender drop off and become part of the coverage, then the end will release and run a hook pattern to the inside at a depth of 8 yards. The primary read for the quarterback is the strong side safety. The ball is thrown opposite the defender's move. On invert action by the safety, the ball is thrown to the split end. If the safety drops straight back or to the outside, the hook pattern to the playside halfback opens. When throwing the hook pattern, the ball is thrown to the outside away from the dropping inside linebacker. The quarterback must watch the angle of drop by the defender. If the pass to the split end and halfback are both covered, then the quarterback will dump the ball to the fullback in the flat.

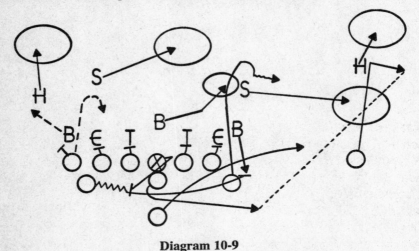

Diagram 10-9

SEMI-SPRINT ACTION

Inside pass patterns off the Sprint or Rollout action requires that the quarterback when moving must pull up short, set up and then throw to the primary receiver. By pulling up, the quarterback is better able to throw the ball opposite the direction in which he is moving. When moving to the outside, and the primary route is an inside pattern such as a curl or post, the quarterback has to throw across his body in a very unnatural movement. Also, by setting up, the quarterback is in a more advantageous position to read the drops of the "underneath" defenders as well as movements by the deep secondary. When pulling up, the quarterback requires a different block on the defensive end. This block has already been mentioned on occasion, the emphasis being that the blocker drive the defensive end to the outside.

JET LEFT SPRINT RIGHT 22

Diagram 10-10 shows a 4-3 defense with man-to-man coverage. Primary patterns to the playside feature both receivers running square out

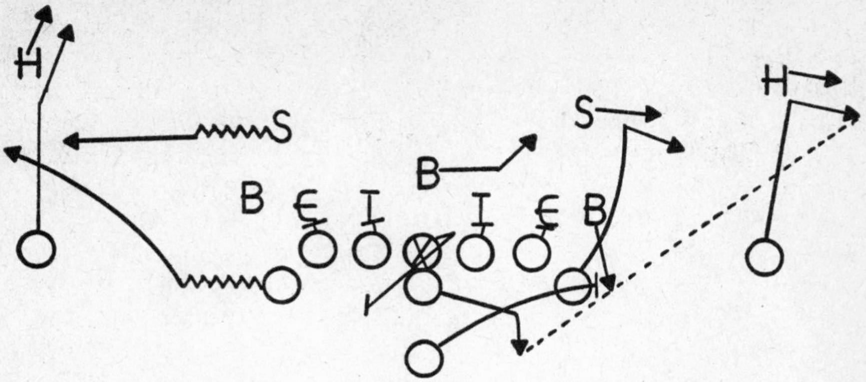

Diagram 10-10

patterns. "Jet" motion is directed to the backside away from the sprint action. The split end to the backside drives into the deep post seam to occupy the defensive halfback on that side. Because of the sprint out action, the linebacker to the playside is responsible for the contain and is blocked to the outside by the fullback. Keys to the playside are based on which receiver is double covered and throwing opposite the doubled receiver. Because of this strategy, it is best for the quarterback to run a semi-sprint technique, providing him with maximum time to read the secondary movements. If the split end receives double coverage, then the halfback should be open in the lane "underneath." Because the outside linebacker plays contain, the middle linebacker must play the halfback should the split end get doubled. Should the halfback be doubled, then the split end will be open. If there are only single man-to-man techniques being played, then the quarterback will throw to whichever receiver gets open first. It is an important coaching point that because of the strict man-to-man coverage, the receivers must accelerate hard when making their cuts. They want to put as much distance as possible between themselves and the defenders once the break is made.

JET LEFT SPRINT RIGHT 95 PICK

Another variation of the semi-sprint (semi-roll) action is illustrated in diagram 10-11. A 3-4 defense (variation of the 5-2 now popular in the Pros) is shown with man-to-man coverage. Pick patterns because of their delays and misdirections are quite effective against man-to-man secondaries. A tight end is aligned to the backside and on the snap drives off to run a hook pattern to the inside at 7 yards. The backside halfback works "jet" motion to the outside, forcing coverage from the defensive halfback to his side. Playside patterns consist of the following strategy: The split end drives off to the outside and then delays. As the ball is snapped, the playside halfback drives to the outside directly at a point 4 yards in front of the split end. When the playside halfback passes in front of the split end, the end will break underneath the halfback, driving hard to the inside running a quick slant or post. Because of the man-to-man techniques, both the safety and halfback make initial moves to the outside. With the split end driving hard to the inside and the safety moving to the outside to play the halfback, a good misdirection situation is created in favor of the split end. The primary receiver is the split end running the delay route. The quarterback sets up and must look quickly for the open lane between the inside safety and linebacker dropping to the hook area.

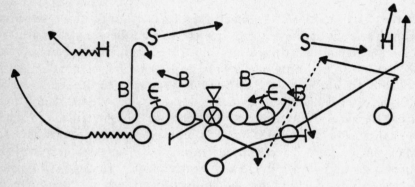

Diagram 10-11

FLY RIGHT SPRINT RIGHT 49 FULLBACK CIRCLE

A 3-man primary pattern with sprint action is shown in diagram 10-12. The fullback becomes the third pass receiver on the playside. The backside halfback becomes responsible for blocking the end defender to the playside. With semi-sprint action, the halfback will block the defensive end to the outside. Primary playside routes include the split end running a curl, the playside halfback working an out-and-up, and the fullback circling over the middle occupying the inside linebacker. The pass route run by the fullback must be effective enough to keep the linebacker out of the throwing lane to the split end on the curl. The quarterback reads the drop of the inside linebacker and throws the ball opposite his movement. Should the linebacker sprint directly to the curl area, then the ball is thrown to the fullback. If the fullback draws man-to-man coverage from the linebacker, the ball is thrown to the split end in the curl lane. In the

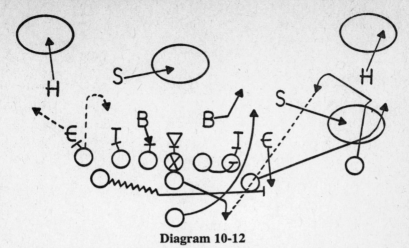

Diagram 10-12

diagram, a 5-2 defense with invert action by the playside safety is shown.
The fullback draws coverage from the inside linebacker, so the ball is delivered to the split end as the lane opens from the inverting safety. On the
backside, the tight end watches for the rush of the defender on or outside
him and because the defender drops into the coverage scheme, the end
releases and runs a hook pattern at 8 yards. An important point for coaching is that the backside guard must check for the rush of the backside
linebacker over him in the 5-2 defense. In the diagram the backer rushes
and is picked up by the backside guard.

THROWBACK STRATEGY
FROM THE SPRINT PASS GAME

Throwback pass action features the quarterback moving to pass in
one direction by means of a sprint out technique, pulling up and throwing
back away from the ball flow. This style of passing attack is designed to
take advantage of defenses that react quickly to ball flow and flood coverage areas to the action side. Because of this quick ball flow and reaction
by the defense, certain areas away from the action now become vacated.
By its alignment and variations, the Double Slot can be a most effective
formation to use in the development of this type of attack. The offense
attacks specific areas away from the play action that are left vulnerable
due to quick rotation by the deep secondary or by linebackers that become
responsible for coverage areas in the direction of ball flow.

Specifically designed patterns must be employed to get the desired
reactions from the secondary when attempting to attack throwback areas.
Diagrams 10-13 and 10-14 illustrate situations where the throwback game

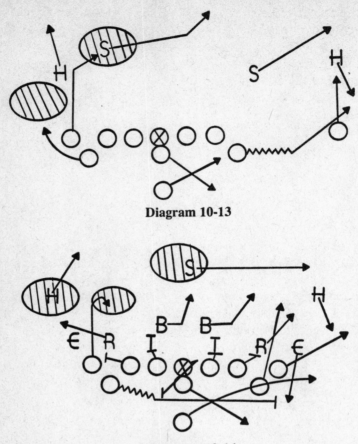

Diagram 10-13

Diagram 10-14

can be effective. The situation in 10-13 features a 4-deep secondary rotating quickly on ball flow. Shaded areas specify vulnerable zones in the secondary as a 4-deep look faces the Double Slot. In diagram 10-14, over-reaction by an inside linebacker from a 4-4 defense leaves the hook zone away from the action side open. The secondary is also rotating in diagram 10-14, leaving the vacated areas as shown.

On all throwback actions, the quarterback will sprint out and set up 6 to 7 yards behind the offensive tackle. Blocking on the playside is the same as for the semi-sprint technique by the quarterback.

FLY RIGHT SPRINTBACK RIGHT 1

Establishing quick rotation in the defensive secondary is essential when throwing back away from the sprint out side. A single man pattern with fast sprint out action is shown in diagram 10-15. The defense is a 4-4 with the secondary and linebackers reacting quickly to ball flow. "Fly" motion is used, and the fullback along with the motioning backside halfback block the defensive end to the play action side. They drive the end defender to the outside providing the quarterback with a maximum protection scheme. Because of the quick flow by the inside linebackers,

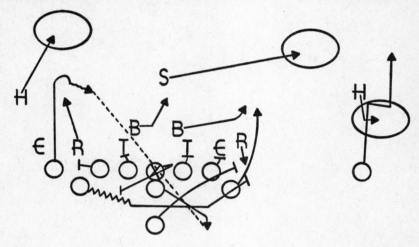

Diagram 10-15

the primary pass pattern is the hook by the tight end. The basic technique is for the receiver to hook and slide opposite the drop of the outside linebacker in a 4-4. The quarterback sprints to a position behind the offensive tackle, sets up, looks to the backside and watches the drop angle of the outside 4-4 linebacker. If the linebacker drops on a flat angle to the outside, then the tight end will be open directly on the hook. Should the outside linebacker work his drop into the hook zone then the quarterback will find the end open sliding to the inside off the hook pattern. The quarterback should have a good idea of defensive coverages he will face to develop effectively the throwback attack. By knowing the coverage types, the quarterback can make an instant read of the primary key and be ready to throw the ball to the intended receiver.

JET RIGHT SPRINTBACK RIGHT 59

A 2-man pattern off the throwback concept is represented in diagram 10-16. Again a 4-4 defense is attacked. "Jet" motion is used to the play action side. As a result the secondary and inside linebackers flow fast as

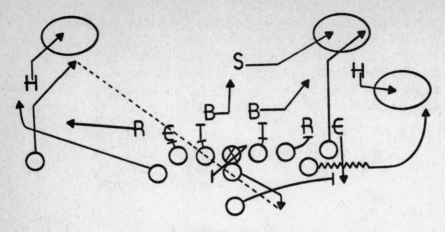

Diagram 10-16

the ball is snapped. Pattern side routes consist of the split end running a deep post working into the deep seam between the defensive halfback and safety. The playside halfback works an out-and-up pattern, drawing man coverage from the outside linebacker. Again the fullback will direct his block to drive the end defender to the outside. The quarterback works a Semi-Sprint technique, sets up and keys the defensive halfback to the pattern side. If the defender hangs or moves to the outside, then the quarterback will throw to the end on the post pattern. If the halfback plays the post tight, then the ball should be thrown to the offensive halfback as he accelerates away from the linebacker.

JET RIGHT SPRINTBACK RIGHT 49

A very similar pass play with the throwback action is shown in diagram 10-17. Again a 2-man pattern is featured with the split end running a curl pattern instead of a post. This play is designed to work against an inside linebacker that does not react quickly flowing on ball action. He actually becomes part of the coverage to the throwback side. A 4-4 defense is again featured with one of the inside linebackers responsible for a designated zone away from the sprint action by the quarterback. Specifically the linebacker works into the throwback lane and helps the backside defensive halfback from underneath. "Jet" motion is used to the sprint side. This forces a compensating move by the middle safety and an adjustment by the outside linebacker to this side. Sprint Out techniques by the fullback and quarterback force one of the inside linebackers to drop off and play the hook zone to the play action side. The remaining inside

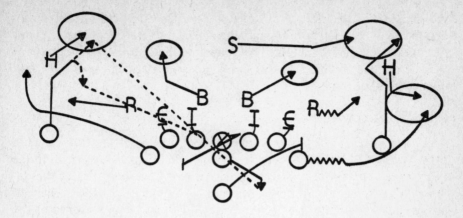

Diagram 10-17

linebacker drops off and becomes part of the coverage to the throwback side. He is the primary key for the quarterback. Playside patterns are the same as in diagram 10-16 except that the split end will now turn the post pattern into a curl, sliding opposite the drop by the inside linebacker. The halfback again runs the out-and-up, drawing single coverage from the outside linebacker. As an alternative, the split end to the pattern side may continue into the post if the inside linebacker is dropping to the curl area most of the time. This situation is shown in diagram 10-17, the split end using the post continuation as an alternate route. The key for the quarterback and split end is as follows: Should the linebacker drop back straight to play the deep 2/3 post seam, then the end will pull up and curl to the inside. If the linebacker uses more of a flat drop to the curl area then the end will continue on into the post. The quarterback must watch the drop angle to throw the long (post) or short (curl) pass.

THROWBACK ACTION AGAINST
4-DEEP SECONDARIES

When attacking 4-deep secondaries, deep zones are less vulnerable due to their occupation by at least 3-deep defenders. Rotation on ball action causes the sprint side deep zones and flat to be covered. In the 4-deep defenses, the "underneath coverages" are comprised of three linebackers, and as a result, short zones to the throwback side are more vulnerable than when there are four linebackers "underneath" as in 8-man front 3-deep defenses. With three linebackers in the short zones, one of them is responsible for an area away from the ball action. The offense should direct pressure at this defender. Releasing two receivers away from sprint action can develop an effective passing strategy to attack this linebacker in the throwback passing areas. The general technique for the quarterback will be to read the drop of this throwback defender and throw the ball opposite his movement.

SPRINTBACK RIGHT 49

Diagram 10-18 shows a 2-man pattern directed away from rotation by a 4-deep 4-3 defense. No motion is used in this play action. Both the quarterback and fullback show sprint action to the right getting the defense to rotate as the ball flows. Pressure is directed to the linebacker opposite flow. The playside split end runs a curl watching the drop of the linebacker. As in the attack on 3-man secondaries, the pattern side halfback runs an out-and-up. The quarterback keys the linebacker. Should the defender move to the playside halfback in the flat, the ball is thrown to the split end on the curl. If the backer drops to help the curl from underneath, then the quarterback hits the halfback as he turns upfield.

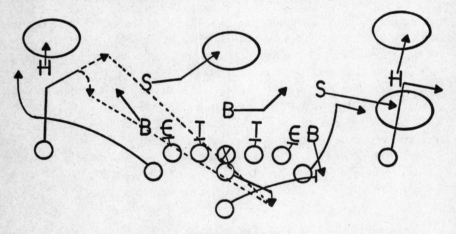

Diagram 10-18

SPRINTBACK RIGHT 22

Similar strategy in attacking a linebacker is represented in diagram 10-19. Here the play is run at the popular 5-2 variation, the 3-4. This defense can include not only a 4-deep secondary, but has at its disposal the potential to drop off four linebackers into the short zones. No motion is again featured. Both receivers to the pattern side run square out routes. If the linebacker drops flat to play the out angle on the split end, the ball is

thrown to the halfback. Should the backer show man-to-man on the
halfback, then the ball is thrown to the split end. If the split end is covered, the ball should be thrown out of bounds.

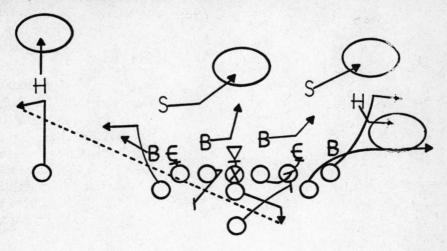

Diagram 10-19

11

Coaching the Double Slot Dropback Pass Game

The dropback passing game from the Double Slot is broken down into two basic phases. Passing strategy is developed within the confines of: first, a strong side attack, and second, passing to the weak side of the formation. Strong side passes consist of those routes run by receivers towards a tight end or motion. Weak side passes are directed away from a tight end and "jet" motion. Field position and hash marks are also considerations when formulating the Dropback attack. In the strong side game both 2- and 3-man pass patterns are developed. To the weak side generally single and 2-man patterns are featured. Protection schemes vary for 2- or 3-man patterns, and emphasis must be placed on the difference in the play calling system.

STRONG SIDE PASS GAME

TWO-MAN PATTERNS

First to be considered in the strong side pass game is the development of 2-man patterns towards a tight end alignment. "Jet" motion is used by the playside halfback to establish a Pro look at the snap of the football. The same pass route numbering system is used as in the Sprint Out pass attack. Because of the 2-man pass route designation, the fullback directs his block towards the pattern side. The fullback checks the first linebacker to the playside and blocks the defender if he rushes. If the linebacker drops into coverage, then the fullback will help the offensive linemen with the blocking. On the backside the halfback will stay in and block if the defender over him rushes. The backside halfback will

release and drive into the deep seam if the defender over him drops into
the coverage. This technique is known as a "flare read" for the halfback.
This same concept would apply also to a tight end if aligned to the
backside.

JET DROPBACK 49

A 2-man pattern is illustrated in diagram 11-1 against the 4-3 defense. In this defensive situation, "invert zone coverage" is developing
towards the tight end, with the linebackers dropping off as compensation
in the "underneath zones." "Jet" motion directs the halfback towards the
outside. On the snap the playside halfback drives downfield and runs a
curl pattern in the seam behind the inverting safety. As the pattern is developed, the halfback must work open away from the drop of the outside

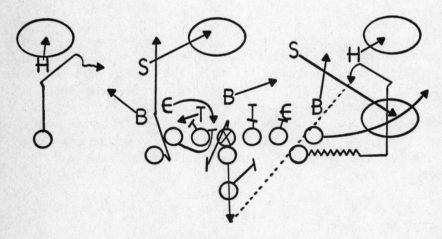

Diagram 11-1

linebacker. The tight end releases wide and runs a "9" pattern into the
deep outside 1/3, drawing coverage from the defensive halfback "zoning" this deep area. As he releases, the tight end reads the safety on invert
action and continues wide working away from the safety's direction. The
fullback checks the middle linebacker, sees the defender drop off into the
coverage and as a result helps the offensive line with their blocking. On
the backside the split end releases and runs a curl route, working the seam
away from the angle of drop by the linebacker. The backside halfback sets
up to block, sees the linebacker over him drop into coverage, releases and
drives into the deep seam between the defensive halfback and safety. The
backside halfback must attempt to draw the linebacker deep out of the curl

throwing lane to the split end. As he drops back, the quarterback concen-
trates on the movements of the strong side safety. Because the safety is
inverting and driving into the flat, the quarterback will look for the
playside halfback on the curl. The second choice for the quarterback will
be the tight end turning upfield. Should the playside safety move to play
the curl or "hang" in position, the quarterback should look to hit the tight
end. In throwing to the tight end, the ball is directed outside and away
from the safety and just behind the halfback rotating into the flat. This
situation off the same pass play is illustrated in diagram 11-2.

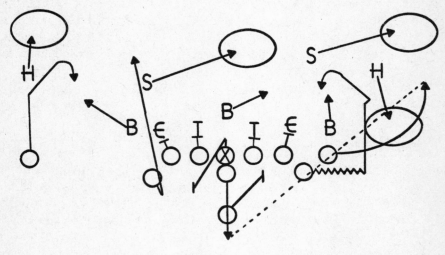

Diagram 11-2

FLY DROPBACK 51 CUP

A pass directed into a split end formation is illustrated in diagram
11-3. This side of the formation is now considered strong as "fly" motion
is shown towards this direction. "Cup" blocking is designated directing
the fullback to block to the backside, reading the technique played by the
first linebacker from the center. The motioning halfback sets up to the
playside and checks the first linebacker to this side for any rush. For both
blockers, if their linebacker becomes involved in the pass rush then he is
blocked. Should the backer drop into coverage, then the halfback or
fullback will help the interior blockers with the rush. A 5-2 defense is
shown that rotates its 4-deep secondary as soon as the "fly" motion
shows. Invert action is used by the playside safety. The split end to the
backside runs a post occupying the deep seam. For the primary pattern, the

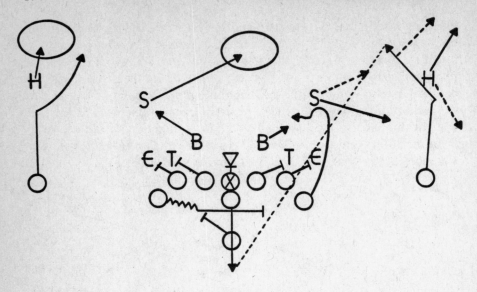

Diagram 11-3

split end runs a post and the halfback hooks. The split end must be ready to adjust his pattern and key the safety. If the safety charges forward show-ing an invert technique, the end continues on the post, working the pattern upfield away from the backside safety. Should the playside safety drop to the post seam, then the end will plant and break away to the outside run-ning a flag. The situation in diagram 11-3 shows the safety inverting, so this will direct the split end to continue on the post technique. The playside halfback releases to the outside and hooks opposite the drop of the inside linebacker. The read for the quarterback is the strong safety. He looks for the split end on the post (or deep on the flag if the safety drops back). The second key for the quarterback is the drop of the inside linebacker to the playside looking for the halfback on the hook and slide technique.

JET DROPBACK 59

Diagram 11-4 illustrates a 2-man pattern against a 4-deep secondary playing man-to-man techniques. The playside halfback runs "jet" motion to the outside. Backside patterns consist of a square out by the split end and a circle route by the halfback (only if the defender over him does not rush). The primary pattern to the playside is a post by the split end. The motion is adjusted to by the secondary sliding over one of its inside safetymen to play the deep flat to the pattern side. Man-to-man coverage

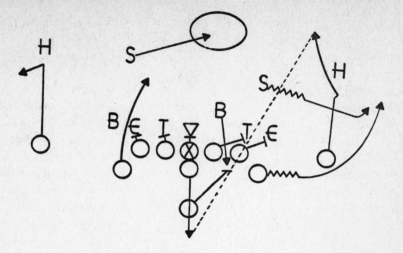

Diagram 11-4

is used on the playside split end. On his release the split end drives off and reads the man-to-man coverage. As he makes his pass cut the end must be sure to accelerate hard, putting himself as far away as possible from the defender. The end must also work away from the backside safety coming over to help out on the post and as a result the post pattern must be directed more upfield. The playside halfback drives wide and upfield, pulling the safetyman outside and away from the throwing lane to the post pattern run by the split end. An inside linebacker to the playside stunts into the line becoming part of the pass rush; he is blocked by the fullback. The quarterback scans the playside looking first for the split end on the post. As a second choice the quarterback will look to the weak side for the halfback on the circle or the split end on the out cut.

FLARE CONTROL

Flare control is a technique where the offensive backs read linebackers and execute a release into pass patterns. The type of release and actual pass route is determined on how the linebacker drops into coverage. Flare control is used primarily in 2-man patterns. Actually it releases a third receiver, but under a more controlled situation. In the Double Slot formation, the fullback is the primary offensive back that is used to carry out flare control. Because of the positioning of the other two halfbacks, they are not in the most advantageous of alignments to read linebackers' reactions. Specific routes that flare control receivers run are directly deter-

mined by the pass route run by the nearest receiver. Should the near receiver run an outside route, then the flare control back will run a circle
pattern to the inside. If the near receiver works an inside route, then the
flare control back will run a swing pattern to the outside.

Examples of flare control by the fullback are illustrated in diagrams
11-5 and 11-6. In diagram 11-5 the playside halfback runs an inside hook
pattern. This causes the fullback to run a swing pattern to the outside.
This only takes place if the linebacker key drops into the coverage. In
diagram 11-6 the playside halfback runs a "9" pattern to the outside. As a
result the fullback now circles to the inside as his key (the outside
linebacker) drops into coverage. The fullback must force the linebacker to
cover him, opening the throwing lane to the split end running a curl.

With "fly" motion and "cup" protection, one of the halfbacks can
be worked into position to execute a flare control technique. Possibilities
of running flare control to both sides exist when using this motion and
blocking scheme. In the "cup" blocking call the fullback directs his block
to the weak side, while the halfback directs himself to the pattern side. As
he sets up, the halfback reads the linebacker to his side. If the linebacker
rushes, then the halfback blocks him. Should the linebacker drop into
coverage, then the halfback will flare control according to the pattern run
by the nearest receiver. If flare control is called to both sides then the
fullback must key the technique of the linebacker to his side. Against an
odd man defense (5-2 and 5-3 types) the fullback keys the first linebacker

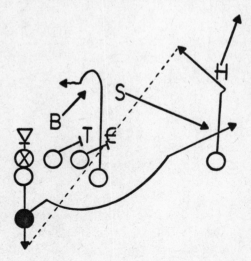

Diagram 11-5

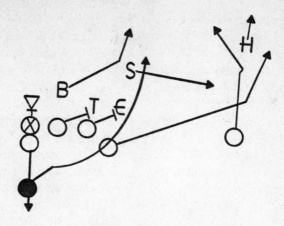

Diagram 11-6

from the center. When facing an even defense (4-3 and 4-4 types) the fullback keys the first backer outside the tackle. The fullback's reactions are the same if the key rushes—block him; if the defender drops off— flare opposite the route of the near receiver.

Diagram 11-7 shows "cup" protection with the halfback executing flare control to the primary pattern side. The split end runs a curl while the playside halfback an out-and-up. Because the playside halfback is run-

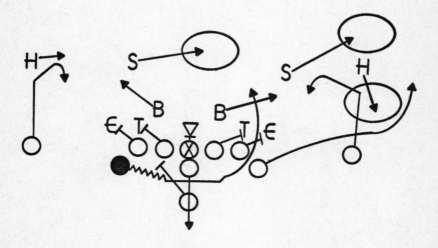

Diagram 11-7

ning an outside pattern by design, the flare control halfback runs an inside circle route if his keys dictate. The flare control back occupies the spot vacated by the inside linebacker that has dropped off "underneath" the curl area. The defensive secondary is playing a corner force scheme. Because of the drop by the linebacker and with the strong safety helping on the curl, the flare back should be open on the circle pattern.

THREE-MAN PATTERNS

The following series of diagrams illustrate various 3-man patterns from the Double Slot Dropback passing game. Placing three men into the pattern can be achieved in a number of ways. The following are some general guidelines to follow when using the Double Slot formation.

1) On the pattern side a tight end, "jet" motion and the fullback releasing on a predetermined pattern call. Diagram 11-8.
2) On the pattern side a split end, "fly" motion and the fullback releasing. Diagram 11-9.

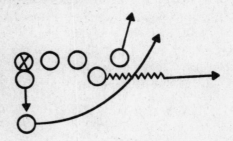

Diagram 11-8

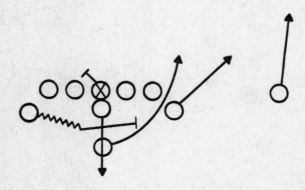

Diagram 11-9

3) Any formation with "motion" by the backside halfback and then being included in the pattern. Diagram 11-10.

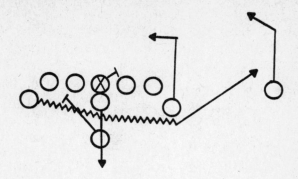

Diagram 11-10

For 3-man patterns the fullback must direct his block to the weak side. The offensive center when facing an even man front must adjust his block to read the technique of the first linebacker to the playside.

HOT RECEIVER

When running 3-man patterns, the Double Slot is vulnerable to stunts by linebackers, especially to the pattern side. This is due primarily to the fact that the fullback is directing his block to the backside with the center compensating to the playside against even man defenses. Generally the center is in a poor position to pick up a blitz by a linebacker outside the offensive tackle. The center will have a most difficult time if one of the outside linebackers does rush from the playside. The area vacated by these rushing linebackers can be effectively occupied by either a tight end or halfback releasing on the primary pattern side. These receivers become "hot" in that the quarterback may dump the ball to them quickly should the linebacker rush to the playside. As the ball is snapped the quarterback reads the movement of the linebacker (it is the middle linebacker in the 4-3 and the first linebacker to the pattern side in other defenses). If the linebacker stunts into the line or vacates away from the playside, then the ball will be thrown to the "hot" receiver.

As he releases, the "hot" receiver reads the linebacker and if the defender rushes or drops away, the receiver will yell, "Hot, hot, hot!" alerting the quarterback to his being open. Diagrams 11-11 and 11-12 show examples of the "hot" receiver concept applied in two defensive situations. In diagram 11-11 the 5-2 linebacker drops away from the pattern side and the quarterback throws to the playside halfback. A middle linebacker from a 4-3 defense stunts into the line in diagram 11-12 and the ball is delivered to the tight end.

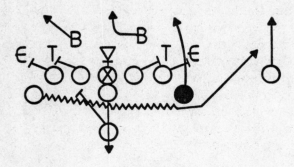

Diagram 11-11

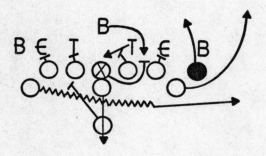

Diagram 11-12

THREE-MAN PATTERNS

In diagrams 11-13 and 11-14 sample play actions illustrate the execution of 3-man pass patterns to the strong side.

MOTION DROPBACK 202

Diagram 11-13 shows a tight end formation to the left. The split end side becomes strong as the backside halfback goes in long "motion" across the formation. The motioning halfback becomes the number 3 receiver in the pattern. Because of the 3-man designation, the fullback directs his block to the backside. A 4-3 defense is shown with "invert" pre-rotation by the secondary as "motion" shows. The front 4 of the defense show a "twist" stunt to the backside. Playside patterns consist of square in routes by the split end and playside halfback. The backside halfback comes off "motion" and drives into the flat. The split end on his release reads the zone move by the strong safety. On his cut the end must "throttle down" in the vacant area behind the defender. The playside halfback works open between the drops of the linebackers at approximately 8 yards. On the backside the tight end runs a hook route working against the outside linebacker to his side. Flare control is executed by the fullback, and because the weak side linebacker is rushing, the fullback blocks him. The quarterback reads the strong safety and looks for one of the playside receivers to be open in a vacated area. Should the strong safety drop to the outside or straight back, then the quarterback will look for the playside halfback over the middle. If the safety runs into the flat (invert action), the quarterback looks for the split end in between the linebacker drops or the backside halfback running away from the inverting safety.

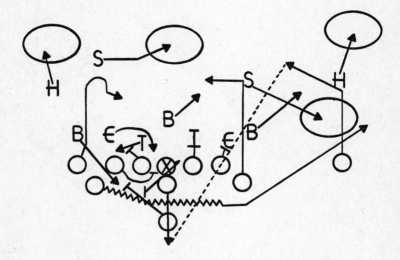

Diagram 11-13

MOTION DROPBACK 528

A double stunt from a 4-4 defense is shown in diagram 11-14. Both inside linebackers blitz through the guard-center gaps. The center blocks the rushing playside linebacker while the fullback takes the backside linebacker. The backside halfback goes in motion and draws coverage from the safety. The motion side halfback is covered by the outside linebacker to his side. Because the defense is in man-to-man coverage techniques, offensive receivers should run patterns that accelerate them away from the defenders. Motion side routes feature a post by the split end and a square out by the motioning halfback. The split end's pattern pulls him away from the coverage of the defensive halfback, while the square out by the offensive halfback puts him some distance from the safetyman. The motion side halfback runs right at the goal post into the vacated area of the middle safety. Since the motion side halfback is now isolated on a linebacker, the resulting mismatch should work out in favor of the offensive player. Before the snap the quarterback watches for any reaction by the secondary to the motion. If the safety chases as illustrated, then the primary receiver will be the halfback in the deep middle. If the safety stays in position, then the quarterback will look to the split end on the post or the "motioning" halfback working into the flat. If the safety rotates on ball action, then the quarterback should look again to the motion side halfback over the middle.

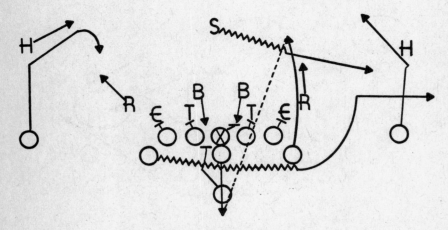

Diagram 11-14

MOTION DROPBACK 502 "HOT"

Use of the "hot" receiver concept is illustrated in diagram 11-15. Also included in the play call is the assigning of the fullback to flare control the backside. The fullback will swing to the outside if his key drops into coverage. The reason for the outside pattern by the fullback is because the tight end on the backside is running a hook pattern to the inside. On the playside the halfback watches the first linebacker to his inside. If the defender rushes, then the halfback becomes the "hot" receiver and looks for the quick pass from the quarterback. Should the linebacker not stunt, then the halfback will run a hook at 8 yards, working opposite the drop angle of the linebacker. The split end works the post while the "motioning" halfback drives into the flat. While running the post, the split end must be ready to readjust his pattern according to how the strong safety reacts. If the safety shuffles back or to the outside, then the receiver will break down into a curl pattern in front of the defender. As the ball is snapped, the backside halfback breaks off his "motion," driving into the flat making adjustments by reading the coverage. If the defense plays a deep flat coverage, then the back will run shallow to the line, keeping away from the safety and halfback. Should one of the defenders rotate up into the flat, then the receiver will work into the seam between the two rotating defenders. Reads and reactions for the quarterback break down into the following series of reactions: First, the quarterback will key the playside linebacker looking for the quick pass to the "hot" receiver. If the linebacker does not stunt, the quarterback switches his read to the strong safety on the pattern side. If the safety moves forward, then the quarterback will look for the split end on the post pattern. If the safety hangs, drops or slides outside, then the quarterback will hit the split end adjusting his pattern to the curl. The quarterback reads from the pattern side to the backside, watching the movement of the defense and offense.

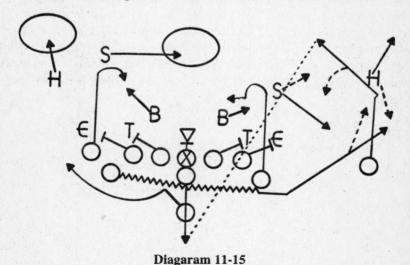

Diagaram 11-15

WEAK SIDE DROPBACK PASSES

Essentially these pass plays are directed away from a tight end or away from motion. When calling weak side patterns, the alignment of the tight end will determine which side of the formation is designated as weak. In a tight end formation, weakside will be away from the tight end's alignment. This phase of the passing attack is designed to throw the ball at defenses that have prepared their coverage calls to the strong side (or motion side) of the formation. Often the split end to the weak side is left in single coverage with defensive halfback. Anytime this occurs, the offensive end has the advantage. Single coverage usually is the result of some predetermined rotational call to the strong side, leaving minimal coverage on the weak side. Some defenses will have predetermined coverages to the weak side, when they suspect the offense may pass the football that way. Weak side passes are also designed to combat these weak side coverages.

ATTACKING THE WEAK SIDE
WITH A SINGLE RECEIVER

With various strong side rotational coverage schemes, the chances are pretty good that the split receiver to the weak side will be effectively isolated in single coverage with the defensive halfback. In attacking the weak side coverage, it is essential to get the offensive receiver in single coverage deep. This is easy with the Double Slot formation. By directing motion towards the strong side, pre-rotation by the defensive secondary shows early. At most the defensive halfback to the weak side will play the split receiver man-to-man with help from the drop of a linebacker working into the out cut from underneath. The defender may also receive late assistance from the weak side safety after the defender has rotated to the deep middle 1/3.

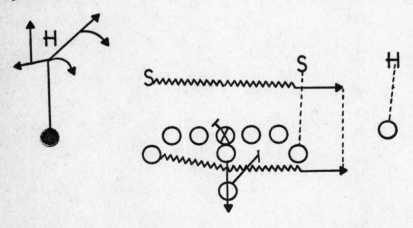

Diagram 11-16

Diagram 11-16 shows "motion" by the halfback with the weak side safety chasing the motion all the way across the formation. This leaves single coverage on the split end. Various pass routes can be run effectively by the split end. Most of the patterns will be determined by the initial position that the weak side defender plays on him. Should the defensive halfback shade inside, then out cuts are in order. If the defender plays outside leverage look to work inside routes. When running the inside routes, the offense must be ready to observe help from inside defenders as the outside alignment by the defensive halfback is designed to funnel the receiver to the inside coverage.

WEAK SIDE PASS ATTACK 2 RECEIVERS

To establish a 2-man weak side attack, the halfback must be brought into the pattern call as the second receiver. In diagram 11-17 a tight end formation with "jet" motion is illustrated. This side is now considered strong because of the tight end alignment and motion technique directed to this side. In 2-man patterns, the fullback directs his block to the called pattern side, in this case away from the tight end and motion. The fullback may also be designated to execute flare control, becoming in effect a 3-man pattern. On the two receiver patterns the offensive center checks the backside linebacker against even defenses and blocks the middle guard when faced with an odd man front. An important block to the backside is that of the tight end. He checks the number of potential rushers aligned outside the offensive tackle. If there are two defenders and both rush, then the end will block the widest one. Should the widest defender drop off into pass coverage, then the tight end releases and runs a

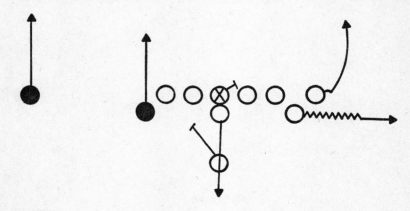

Diagram 11-17

hook pattern at 8 yards, watching the drop by the linebacker. This is a
flare control read for the tight end.

JET RIGHT DROPBACK WEAK 21 FLARE CONTROL

A 4-4 defense is being passed against in diagram 11-18. On the pattern side the split end runs a square out at 12 yards. The playside halfback
runs a hook turning to the inside. He must slide opposite the drop of the
inside linebacker. The fullback blocks to the pattern side and executes
flare control opposite the pattern run by the halfback (the fullback swings
outside because the halfback runs an inside curl). On the backside the
halfback runs "jet" motion giving the formation a Pro look. The tight end
reads the rush. The outside linebacker to the backside drops into coverage
so the tight end releases and runs a square in adjusting the route to the
angle of drop by the inside linebacker. The motioning halfback drives
downfield and runs a curl route working around the drop of the outside
linebacker. On the dropback the quarterback reads the weak side, looking
for the split end on the out cut and, as a second choice, the hooking
halfback. The fullback, running the flare control route, or the split end
should be open due to the flooding zone effect in this pattern design. As a
last choice the quarterback will scan for the tight end or motioning
halfback to the strong side.

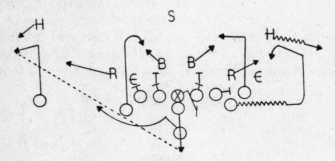

Diagram 11-18

THREE-MAN PATTERNS TO THE WEAK SIDE

Successful 3-man pass routes can also be run to the weak side. The
fullback becomes the third man involved in the pattern. "Jet" motion is
used with a tight end away from the pattern side. To many defenses the
positioning of a tight end and motion to the same side creates a strong
formation. The secondary may rotate this way on ball action (drop back or
sprint out strong) or pre-rotate when any motion shows.

JET RIGHT DROPBACK WEAK 51 FB SWING

Diagram 11-19 shows a 3-man pattern directed to the weak side. The secondary shows a weak rotation call and revolves its coverage this way on dropback action. In this coverage scheme the defensive halfback rotates up and levels in the weak side flat. The weak safety sprints to the deep outside 1/3. The strong safety drives to the deep middle, while the remaining defensive halfback to the strong side zones the deep outside 1/3. The fullback is the third receiver in the pattern and he runs a swing route opposite the inside pattern of the playside (weak side) halfback. The pattern for the playside halfback is to run an inside hook designed to slide opposite the drop of the near linebacker. With the middle linebacker in a 4-3 defense dropping to the strong side, an area opens where the weak side halfback sits and watches for the quarterback to throw him the ball.

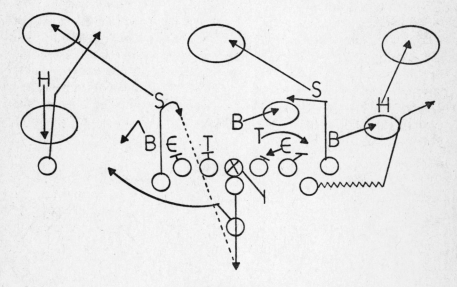

Diagram 11-19

When running the swing route, the fullback gains depth which gives him some maneuverability if the ball is thrown to him. Backside patterns consist of the tight end running a square in getting open in the seam opposite the linebacker drops. On his release the tight end has reacted to his flare control key. Because one of the rushers drops off, the end will automatically release on a pattern. The motioning halfback comes off the "jet" technique and runs a square out at 8 yards. For the quarterback, he watches the drop of the middle linebacker. If the linebacker drops into the pattern side, then the quarterback looks for the tight end on the square in. The diagram shows the linebacker dropping to the strong side so the quarterback now directs the throw to the pattern side, the halfback running the hook route. The remaining outside linebacker to the playside covers the fullback man-to-man. This maneuver keeps the throwing lane to the playside halfback open. The final choice for the quarterback is the fullback. The ball will be thrown to him if the playside halfback draws coverage from the outside linebacker to the pattern side.

JET RIGHT DROPBACK WEAK 62 FB FLAT

Another variation of the weak 3-man pattern is shown in diagram 11-20. In this play two split ends are deployed with "jet" motion directed outside one of them. A weak rotation coverage scheme is shown by the defense. The playside halfback becomes a "hot" receiver and uses the "hot" read keys. Playside patterns for the split end and fullback consist of a flag by the end working away from the rotating inside safety and the fullback driving into the flat. For the quarterback the primary pattern is the split end on the flag. Should the weak side safety show invert, then the split end should adjust his pattern to a post, staying away from the safety rotating to the deep middle. The pass should be directed opposite the move of the weak safety, either the flag or post.

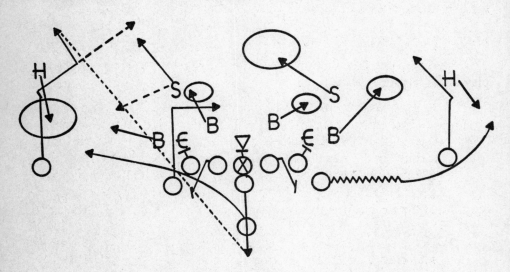

Diagram 11-20

12

Coaching Double Slot Play Action and Screen Passes

The number and variety of running plays in the Double Slot offense allows the development of a most effective play action pass game. In all these passes the run dimension must be convincingly faked as an initial movement. With the running threats presented by options, power sweeps, traps and counters, the defense can be effectively attacked by passing the football. Areas vacated by the defense can be exploited as defenders commit themselves to the run fake. As a result both the running and passing games begin to complement one another in their effectiveness.

ADVANTAGES OF PLAY ACTION PASSES

The following is a list of offensive advantages gained when running play action passes:

1) A good fake by the quarterback of the running play holds the linebackers to their individual "run keys." Playside offensive linemen fire out on the snap so that defensive linemen will react to playing the run first. A good run fake also has a controlling effect on the pass rush. Defensive linemen play a more cautious game in passing situations. A good run fake also delays the drops of the linebackers into the short zones, enhancing the effectiveness of the short passing game.

2) Delay of the pass delivery disrupts the timing in the defensive secondary. Defenders are forced to respect and play the run threat first, before adjusting to their coverage areas. This gives the pass receiver a greater advantage as he runs his individual route.

3) After the ball fake, the quarterback may set up or roll out in

either direction, breaking many keys for the defense as to from where the pass will be actually thrown.

4) Play action passes place good control on the defensive rush. Offensive linemen to the playside must fire out to simulate a running play. Because of the fire out technique, defensive linemen not only react to and play run, but any pass rush lanes that they may have pre-established become disrupted. Defensive linemen do not know exactly from what point the pass will be thrown. Rushing angles to the quarterback change on the run as the play action develops.

5) With good fakes into the line, various backs can slip out into the pattern. Because of the delayed reaction to the pass in the secondary, potential receivers can work into their patterns more effectively before any pre-called coverage develops.

VEER ACTION PASSES

The most common and popular running play in the Double Slot is the Fullback Veer play with the various option dimensions run from the initial fake to the fullback. Most effective play action passes are those that fake the most frequent running play in as many aspects as possible before the actual ball is delivered. In running Veer action passes, the offense fakes not only the base fullback play but also the option. Initial movements by the offensive players must simulate the option play in as many phases as possible. Key points in the play involve:

1) A good ride fake to the fullback that holds the inside linebacker(s). This delays their drops into the short passing zones.

2) After the disconnect, the quarterback works down the line as if to option the defensive end with a pitch or keep. This phase of the play action is carried out for two steps. The quarterback then drops back to 7 yards and reads the defense.

3) Depth of the quarterback may vary depending on the types and length of pass routes that receivers run. The pass will be delivered rather quickly if short zones are to be attacked. If receivers are running deep routes, then the quarterback will take a maximum drop, allowing the most time for the route to be run by the receiver. The option fake is essential to place maximum run read on the defense.

INDIVIDUAL TECHNIQUES
FOR THE VEER ACTION PASS

Playside end—Run the called pass route. Initial release and movements must simulate the stalk block technique of the option.

Playside linemen—Aggressive controlled blocking giving the defense as much of a run look as possible.

Playside Tackle—Block the man on or the first defender to the outside. Drive through the defender's outside hip, moving him off the ball. If facing the 5-2 defense and the tackle slants hard to the inside, pick up the linebacker stunting around.

Playside Guard—Against the 5-2, step at the defensive tackle at a 45-degree angle. Be controlled so that a stunting defender can be blocked. Block the linebacker if he shoots. Should the defensive tackle slant down hard to the inside, drive him off the line of scrimmage as deep as possible. If there is no stunt by the tackle, pull around the offensive tackle and set up just outside him. Against an even defense, and covered as in the 4-3 and 4-4 defenses, fire out through the outside hip of the defender, stay under control and drive him off the line of scrimmage.

Center—Against the 5-2 and 5-3 defenses, work the same initial steps as in the Fullback Veer running play. Drive block through the playside hip of the middle guard. If uncovered, step back to the playside and watch for the drop of the middle linebacker; be ready for a stunt and block the linebacker if he loops around the defensive tackle to the playside. If no stunt develops turn to the backside and help block the rush.

Backside guard—As with the offensive center, execute the Veer play for the first few steps. Against the 5-2 defense the linebacker playing over must be given a run fake key. Step at the middle guard and help the center with his block if the defender is escaping to the backside. If the middle guard is blocked (or slants to the playside) check the linebacker over for a blitz. As a last technique, set back off the line and help with the rush coming from the outside. If faced with an even defense and covered, Hinge block the defender.

Backside tackle—Execute the hinge technique.

Backside end—If tight, hinge or release into the pattern depending on the call.

Playside halfback—"Arc" release and work into the seam between the deep outside 1/3 defender and the defender responsible for the pitch. Get into this area before making the final pass cut. "Arc" will give an option key to the defensive secondary.

Fullback—Fake the Veer and *get tackled* by the linebacker. If untouched drive to a depth of 7 yards and curl in the open area between the linebacker drops.

Backside halfback—Use "fly" motion. Work for a pitch relationship with the quarterback. Attack and block the defensive end.

Quarterback—Fake the Veer. Work two steps into the option. Drop back 6 to 7 yards, read the defense and throw the primary pass cut.

The following diagrams illustrate the Veer action pass in various defensive situations. In calling the play the same two digit number is used to designate the playside routes. In addition to the number a play action description is called. For example, the huddle call for diagram 12-1 would be "Veer Right Action 28."

VEER RIGHT ACTION 28.

In diagram 12-1 a 5-2 defense shows a strong invert rotation by the safety as a reaction to run keys. The primary objective of the safety is to beat the "arc" block of the playside halfback, and tackle the pitchman. On the playside the defensive tackle and linebacker are involved in a "pinch-scrape" stunt. A good Veer fake is made by the fullback along with agressive blocking by the playside offensive linemen.

Playside end—Release and simulate the "stalk" technique. Plant the outside foot and break into the sidelines at a depth of 8 yards.

Playside halfback—"Arc" release and work into the playside seam between the pitch support defender and the deep outside 1/3 defender. In the illustrated situation get behind the forcing safety. Should be wide open as there is no support from the inside linebacker because he is involved in a stunt.

Fullback—Fake the Veer and work into the open space behind the stunting linebacker at a depth of 8 yards. Draw coverage from the backside linebacker, keeping him out of the throwing lane to the playside halfback.

Quarterback—Execute the Veer play. Work the option and drop back to read the defense. The action of the safety is the key. If he inverts, look for the halfback in the seam quickly. The second choice on the invert is the out cut by the split end. Should the safety hang and play the halfback man-to-man, then look to the split end in behind the defensive halfback. If both receivers are covered, look for the fullback on the 8 yard hook.

Backside end—Work into the deep post seam.

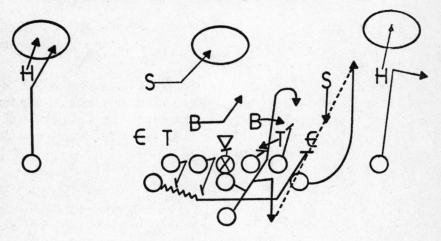

Diagram 12-1

VEER RIGHT ACTION 49

Another Veer action pass is shown in diagram 12-2 with an inside curl pattern by the split end as the feature route. The playside halfback works outside into the flat, turning upfield into the deep outside 1/3. These patterns simulate the "X" call blocking variation used in the running play. A 4-3 defense is shown with invert rotation to the action side by the defensive safety. The middle linebacker reacts initially to stop the veer threat, then reacts to cover the fullback man-to-man. The outside linebacker reacts by first playing the quarterback, as a result he drops to the outside curl throwing lane too late.

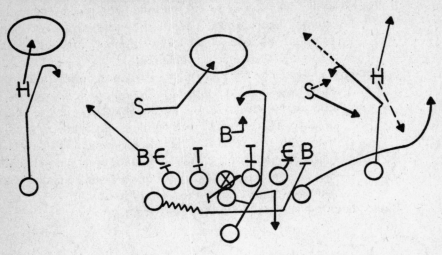

Diagram 12-2

Playside end—Run the curl pattern and watch the reactions of the safety. If the safety shows invert, curl and hang in the open lane. Should the safety cover the curl area the end will drive into the post.

Playside halfback—On the release, watch the safety. If the defender plays back, then drive into the seam between the safety and halfback. With the safety showing invert, work wide into the flat to draw the defender from the throwing lane to the split end.

Quarterback—Make a super but very patient fake. Set up at a depth of 7 yards and read the movements of the safety. On invert action, throw to the split end curling. If the safety hangs to cover the curl, dump the ball to the halfback in the flat. When looking to throw to the halfback, the ball must be thrown in between the defensive halfback and safety if there is hard corner rotation. If the corner is "soft," throw as the halfback turns upfield. The outlet receiver is again the fullback.

Fullback—Run the hook pattern but in this situation turn to the inside, working away from the drop angle of the linebacker. The reason for the inside turn is to keep the throwing lane open to the split end.

VEER RIGHT ACTION 59 PICK

A successful pick pattern from the Veer play action is illustrated in diagram 12-3. The defense is a 4-4 with man-to-man coverage on the receivers. The middle safety is free to play the ball while the playside receivers are covered by the outside linebacker and defensive halfback. On the backside the split end runs a deep post getting into the seam drawing the attention of the free safety.

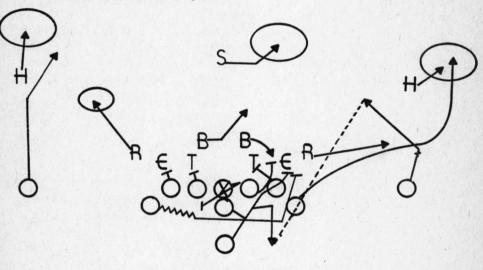

Diagram 12-3

Playside end—Drive off and delay. Wait for the playside halfback to cross to the outside. As the halfback clears, plant and cut to the inside, driving hard on a quick slant or post.

Playside halfback—Release outside and drive directly for a point 4 yards in front of the split end. Work into the outside 1/3, taking the defensive halfback deep.

Fullback—Run the Veer action and help with the blocking up front. Essentially this is a 2-man pattern, so draw a tackle from the linebacker responsible for the Veer.

Backside halfback—Run the option course. Work for the proper pitch relationship to a point behind the playside tackle. Turn upfield and block the defensive end.

Quarterback—Carry out the essential fakes. Drop back and set up. Look for the split end on the quick post. If covered, look to the backside for the split end in the deep seam.

THROWBACK STRATEGY
WITH THE VEER ACTION PASS

Diagram 12-4 illustrates a simple throwback pass off the Veer action fake. The design of the pass is to control areas of the defense that pursue quickly from the backside and outnumber the option to the playside. Two positions are attacked: First, the backside linebacker and, second, the backside safety. The backside linebacker is the first consideration as he frequently flows fast and stops the fullback. Because he flows quickly, it is advantageous for the offense to attack this vacated area with a short pass. This can have an effect of control on the quick flow of this defender. The split end is directed into a curl pattern at the linebacker's vacated spot.

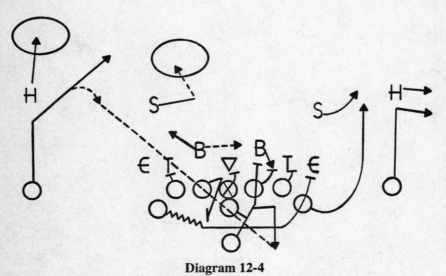

Diagram 12-4

The backside safety will play primarily two types of techniques against option type attacks: He will play reckless and attack the playside immediately on flow. As a second technique he will play a bit more cautious and key the actions of the quarterback. If the safety flows quickly to the playside on ball action, then the split end on the backside should run a post into the vacated seam. If the safety is more cautious and mirrors the action of the quarterback, then the receiver to the backside runs the curl.

Action side pass patterns are a square out by the end, with the halfback "arcing" into the seam.

The situation in 12-4 shows the safety watching the quarterback movements and the backside linebacker flowing fast to the action side. As a result the quarterback hits the split end running the curl pattern to the inside.

A similar situation is illustrated in 12-5. Here a 4-4 defense is flowing quickly with its safety and linebackers. Because the safety is moving quickly to the action side on ball flow, the pass is thrown to the split end on the post.

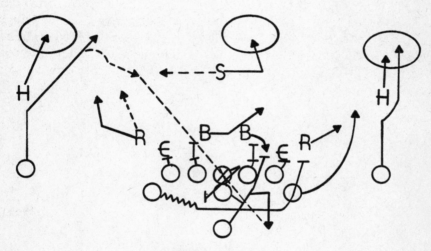

Diagram 12-5

SLANT ACTION PASSES

The passes in this category are based on the off-tackle play with the backside halfback coming off motion as the ball carrier. As many aspects of the slant play must be emphasized as possible. This includes the playside guard pulling and blocking the defensive end. For the most part slant action passes are run into a split end to take advantage of the wider passing lanes. When running the play into a tight end, a flooding effect takes place in the short outside defensive zones. Key coaching points for the slant action pass are as follows:

1) The receivers run their patterns 3 to 4 yards deeper because of the time required by the quarterback to carry out the ball fakes.

2) "G" blocking by the playside guard. This pattern is used against the 5-2 defense. The guard hook blocks the defensive end. If the defensive penetrates straight upfield, then the guard will kick the end out.

3) An excellent fake and fill block by the fullback over the playside guard. If there is no stunt by the linebacker, then the fullback will work 7 to 8 yards deep over the position of the playside offensive tackle.

4) **Backside halfback**—Execute a good Slant fake with a block on the end defender.

SLANT RIGHT ACTION 22

The basic Slant action pass into a split end is shown in diagram 12-6.

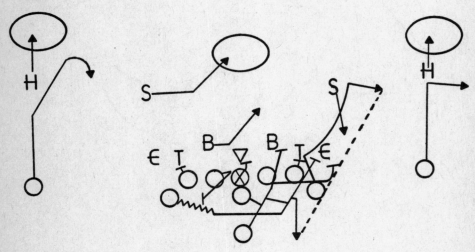

Diagram 12-6

Playside end—Drive deep and break to the outside at 12 yards.

Playside halfback—Fake a block on the defensive tackle and then slide into the seam ("lead" technique). Make a quick fake to the inside and run an out cut at 8 yards.

Fullback—Fake the Veer and fill block for the pulling guard.

Backside halfback—Fake the Slant and help the playside guard block the defensive end.

Backside end—Run a deep post, working in between the rotating defenders.

Quarterback—Fake the Slant in all dimensions. Be patient and don't rush the fakes. Drop back behind the playside tackle and look quickly for the safety. If the safety is in a close support of the line of scrimmage, then hit the playside halfback in behind the defender at 8 yards on the out cut. If the safety is rotating to the outside, then look for the split end in the seam on his out cut.

SLANT RIGHT ACTION 87 TIGHT END DRAG

The play shown in diagram 12-7 is an example of a 3-man pattern from the slant action. The third receiver is a tight end aligned to the backside. His pattern is to run across the formation looking for the hole in the "underneath" coverage at a depth of 12 to 14 yards. The defense is a 4-3, with man-to-man coverage and a "free" safety. Against an "even" defense all linemen fire out on the action side and block the defenders over them. There is no pulling by the playside guard, that technique is used in attacking the 5-2 front.

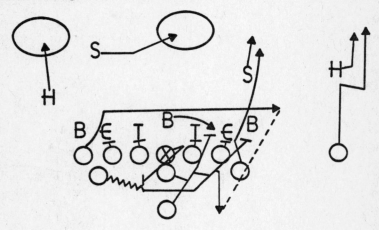

Diagram 12-7

Playside end—Run the out-and-up cut off the sideline pattern. Take the defender as deep as possible.

Playside halfback—Fake a block on the defensive end (4-3 defense). Release and drive into the deep seam drawing the safety all the way.

Backside end—Release to the inside and work completely across the formation. Gain depth to 14 yards. Look for the pass in open area just outside the original position of the playside offensive tackle.

Quarterback—Good slant fakes. Get the correct drop to 7 yards and look for the backside tight end. If the end is covered by the playside safety, then look deep for the playside halfback in the seam.

SLANT RIGHT ACTION 89

An example of running the Slant Action Pass into a tight end is shown in diagram 12-8. In this situation the tight end fakes a down block, releases and breaks into the deep flat. The playside halfback continues to run the seam pattern, drawing coverage from the safety. Because the defense is a 5-2, the playside guard pulls and blocks the defensive end. The guard will receive help from the backside halfback after the slant fake. The quarterback looks for the tight end, and if he is covered, then the ball will be thrown to the halfback down the seam. A good fake block by the tight end should draw the safety towards the line of scrimmage, allowing the playside halfback to work deep into the seam.

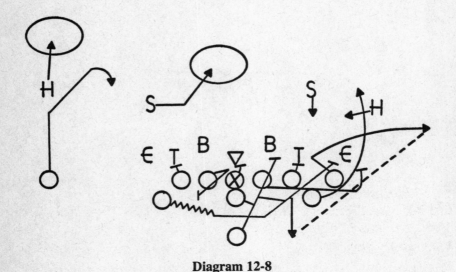

Diagram 12-8

BELLY ACTION PASSES

Play action from the Belly Series can also be adapted to the passing game. The fullback hits wider, aiming for the outside leg of the offensive tackle. The quarterback reverse pivots and fakes to the fullback before dropping back to pass.

BELLY RIGHT ACTION 52

Many of the techniques used in the Veer action passes can be used in the Belly action passes. Diagram 12-9 shows a basic example of a Belly action pass directed at the 4-3 defense. Both receivers run crossing patterns. The split end running a post and the playside halfback sliding into the flat. The quarterback sets up and reads the safety, directing the throw opposite the defender's move. (Invert—throw to curl. Drop back—flat pass to the halfback.)

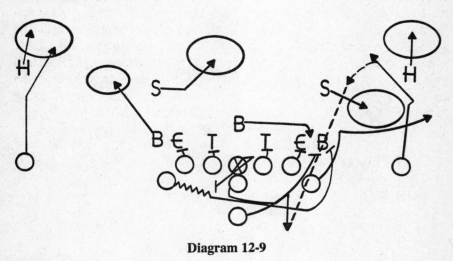

Diagram 12-9

BUCK ACTION PASSES

Buck action passes are derived from the Buck Dive and trap plays that fake the fullback into the line away from the action flow. In diagram 12-10 the pass is directed to the split end side of the formation. The backside halfback fakes the sweep as he comes off of "fly" motion.

BUCK ACTION RIGHT 45

Diagram 12-10 shows Buck action with the primary receiver as the split end. The end runs a curl pattern, sliding opposite the drop angle of the "underneath" coverage. As a secondary pattern, the tight end runs a deep post over the middle. The action side halfback runs the seam cut.

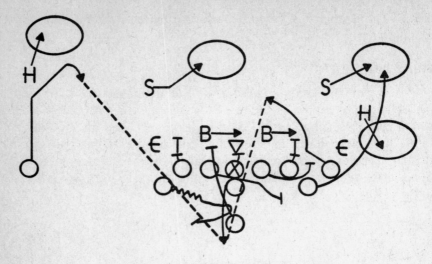

Diagram 12-10

Playside end—Run the curl pattern. Work opposite the angle of drops by the linebackers.

Fullback—Execute Buck action and fill block for the pulling guard.

Playside halfback—Release to the outside and work into the deep 1/3.

Backside halfback—Go in "fly" motion. Pull back and set up to pass block on the backside.

Tight end—Release inside and run a deep post. Work across the field looking for the open areas.

Quarterback—Fake the Buck Dive and Sweep. Drop back and watch the safety to the pattern side. If the safety has flowed to the action side, hit the split end on the curl. If the safety is staying in position to help on the split end coverage, look for the tight end on the deep post.

LEAD ACTION PASSES

These plays are directly derived from option plays that feature the quarterback sliding down the line, reading the defensive end and reacting to the defender's movements with a keep or pitch of the ball. Three examples are considered for the passing game. First, a pass play off the Straight Option, and, second, two examples using the Fullback Option action as a basis. For the most part pass patterns will be the same as for the Veer action passes where option techniques are stressed as initial movements for the offensive players.

STRAIGHT OPTION ACTION RIGHT 28

Diagram 12-11 shows a pass play attacking the 4-4 defense from the Straight Option action. In this situation the quarterback fakes the Sprint out pass for two steps, slides down the line as if to option the defensive end. After moving down the line for three steps, the quarterback drops back and sets up to throw. Both the fullback and backside halfback block the defensive end.

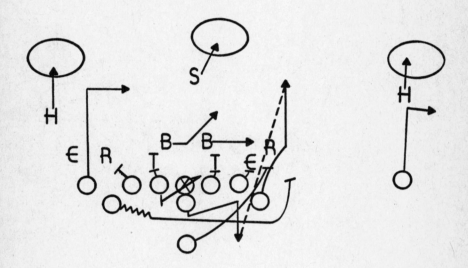

Diagram 12-11

Playside halfback—Release outside and work into the seam.

Playside end—Release and run a square out at 10 yards.

Backside end—Run a square in route at 8 yards.

Quarterback—Fake the Straight Option for at least three steps. Drop back and watch the drop of the outside linebacker. If the defender covers the playside halfback, then the ball is thrown to the out cut by the split end. Should both the playside halfback and end be covered, then the quarterback will look to the backside end running the square in.

FULLBACK OPTION ACTION
"MOTION" RIGHT 798

A pass play with the Fullback Option as a basis is illustrated in diagram 12-12 against the 3-4 defense. Long "motion" directs the backside halfback across the formation. A 3-man pattern develops to the passing side.

Playside end—Drive off deep and run the sideline and go pass route.

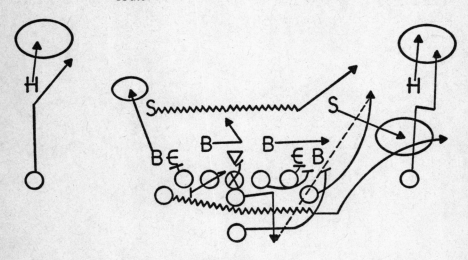

Diagram 12-12

Playside halfback—Use the "arc" release and work into the playside seam.

Backside halfback—Go in long "motion" and drive into the playside flat.

Fullback—Work for a pitch relationship with the quarterback. Cut up and attack the defensive end blocking the defender inside or outside depending on his angle of penetration.

Quarterback—Work down the line for three steps and then drop back to 7 yards. As the "motion" develops, watch the adjustment by the secondary. If the playside safety adjusts by moving to the flat, then look to hit the halfback in the seam. Should the safety move back and to the outside, hit the playside end on the deep go pattern. If "motion" is chased all the way by the backside safety, then on the snap the quarterback will look to the backside split end running the post.

JET RIGHT FULLBACK OPTION LEFT 68

The same play action as shown in diagram 12-12 develops in diagram 12-13, with the exception that the play action is directed opposite the direction of the "jet" motion. A 4-deep 4-3 defense compensates by taking the action side defenders and playing them man-to-man on the offensive receivers to their side. On the motion side the safetyman moves into the flat while the defensive halfback plays the split end man-to-man.

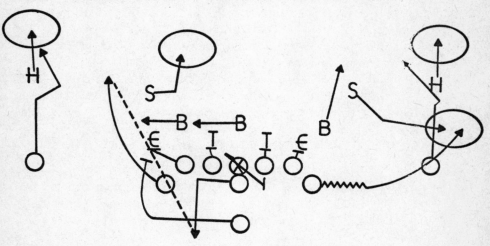

Diagram 12-13

On man-to-man coverage, receivers must remember to accelerate hard on their cuts, to put as much distance as possible between themselves and the defenders covering them.

    Playside end—Run a deep flag pattern off an initial post technique.

    Playside halfback—Release outside ("arc" technique) and run down the seam. If the safety frequently drops to cover this pattern, then the same play action will be shown but the ball will be pitched to the fullback making the play a run.

    Fullback—Run the option path. Cut up and block the defensive end.

    Backside end—Work into the deep post seam, accelerating away from the defensive halfback.

Quarterback—Run the option course. Drop back and read the action of the playside safety. If the safety hangs or drops straight back, look for the split end at the corner of the end zone (depending on field position). Should the safety move forward, dump the ball to the halfback in the seam.

BOOTLEGS

The plays in this series feature a misdirection in the backfield with quarterback sprinting or rolling out opposite the flow, reading a defensive key and throwing the football. The misdirection is designed to get the defense to rotate towards flow and then throw back into areas left vacant by their coverage schemes. Also the linebackers are influenced to play the run first before moving to their "underneath" coverage assignment. Bootlegs are run from three backfield actions. First, from the Power Sweep with the fullback leading. Second, from Buck action with the fullback filling to the actual playside. Third, from the most frequent run action in the offense, in this case the Veer.

POWER SWEEP BOOTLEG LEFT 6 TIGHT END DRAG

The Bootleg pass off the power sweep action is shown in diagram 12-14. The defense is a 5-2 with the secondary and linebackers rotating on flow. The quarterback fakes a hand-off to the halfback, then slides to the outside, looking for a receiver in the open hole in the defense at 14 yards.

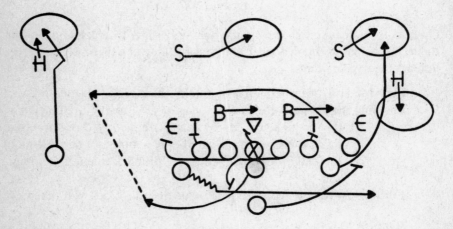

Diagram 12-14

Playside end—Run a flag off the initial post technique.

Playside halfback—"Fly" motion and fake the Power Sweep to the backside.

Backside halfback—Release outside and run the seam cut.

Backside end—Align in a tight position. Fake block to the inside for a single count. Release and "drag" across the field, working for a depth of 12 to 14 yards over the position of the playside halfback.

Guards—Pull to the playside. On the playside, hook the end to the inside. The backside guard peels back behind the original position of the playside guard.

Fullback—Lead the play action to the backside.

Quarterback—Look for the secondary reaction to "fly" motion. If the safety moves to the deep middle, the play has a good chance. Fake the sweep hand-off to the playside halfback. Gain depth and set up. Look for the tight end coming across at a depth of 12-14 yards.

BUCK ACTION BOOTLEG LEFT 6
FULLBACK FLAT (WAGGLE)

Diagram 12-15 is another Bootleg play featuring the fullback sliding into the playside flat after his fake into the line. The split end runs the flag route while the backside tight end drives into the deep post seam. The quarterback fakes the dive, fakes the sweep, rolls left and looks to hit the fullback in the flat. A 5-2 defense is shown with the linebackers and sec-

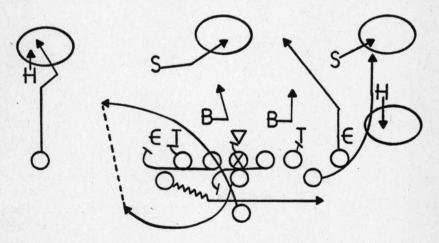

Diagram 12-15

ondary flowing towards the play action side. The offensive guards execute the same technique as for the Bootleg play off the power sweep action.

VEER RIGHT ACTION BOOTLEG
LEFT 6 HALFBACK DRAG

A Bootleg based on the Veer running play is shown in diagram 12-16. Here the quarterback makes an excellent ride fake to the fullback, pivots back and sprints opposite the flow. The playside end (tight) releases and runs a flag (or to the corner), while the backside halfback releases to the inside and drags across the formation working for a depth of 12-14 yards. A 3-4 defense is diagrammed with the secondary double covering the split end and zone rotation to the playside. Because the playside safety reacts to the flow of the Veer fake (this is enhanced as a result of the option game), the quarterback should look for the backside halfback working across into the open area. The backside guard will pull opposite the action flow and block the end defender to the playside.

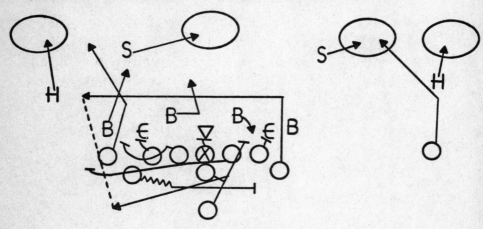

Diagram 12-16

SPECIAL PASSES

In this category of pass plays fall halfback passes. These plays feature the backside halfback becoming the passer with a predetermined receiver. Halfback passes will feature the following initial backfield actions. The pass will be thrown from the option based on an initial Veer fake to the fullback. After a good fake of the Buck Sweep the ball carrier will look to hit the tight end in the flat. This is the second basic halfback action pass. As a third alternative the play is run off the Power Sweep. Here the halfback looks to hit a receiver in the playside seam or some sort of a drag pattern by a backside receiver.

HALFACK OPTION PASS RIGHT

Here is the play that makes the option much more effective. In diagram 12-17 the initial Veer action is faked with the quarterback deliberately pitching the ball. The backside halfback takes the pitch and looks to hit the playside halfback working in the seam or the split end running the deep sideline and go pattern. The diagram shows the playside safety rotating forward to cover the pitch dimension of the play and as a result the ball is thrown to the halfback in the seam.

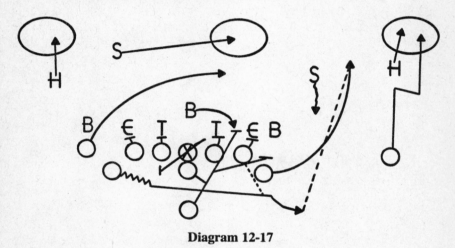

Diagram 12-17

BUCK SWEEP RIGHT HALFBACK PASS

In diagram 12-18 the halfback pass is again illustrated, but in this situation Buck action is faked with the quarterback handing the ball to the halfback.

Tight end—Step to the inside at a 45-degree angle. Release straight upfield and drive into the flat at a depth of 10 yards.

Playside halfback—Release outside the defensive end and drive straight upfield in the seam between the safety and defensive halfback.

Fullback—Execute the Buck Dive and fill block for the pulling backside guard.

Backside halfback—Run the Buck Sweep action. Receive the handoff from the quarterback and gain depth to 5 yards. Look for the tight end to be open in the flat. If the defense is staying back playing pass, then run with the football.

Backside end—Run a deep post in between the rotating deep secondary.

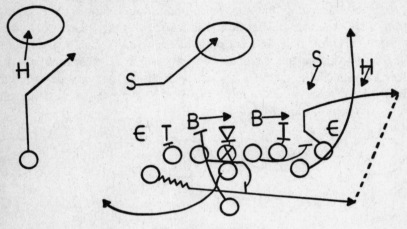

Diagram 12-18

Quarterback—Execute the Buck Sweep. Carry out a Bootleg fake opposite the play action.

POWER SWEEP RIGHT HALFBACK PASS

The halfback pass is again illustrated in diagram 12-19 from Power Sweep action. The defense is a 4-4 with a 3-deep secondary playing a "locked in" zone coverage. Power sweep action is shown by the backfield. In the illustrated situation the halfback is looking for the backside tight end dragging across the formation as the primary receiver. If the tight end is covered, then the halfback will look to throw to the playside halfback driving deep down the seam. All remaining positions fake the Power Sweep.

END AROUND PASS

The final play in the "special" pass category is the End Around Pass off the Veer Option play action. Diagram 12-20 illustrates the Veer Option play with the pitch made to the split end coming back around to the other side of the formation. As in the End Around running play, the action must look as if the split end has intercepted the pitch of the quarterback. Offensive linemen to the playside carry out their initial movements as for the End Around running play, but because the action is a pass they must stay on the line of scrimmage as they slide to the outside. The playside

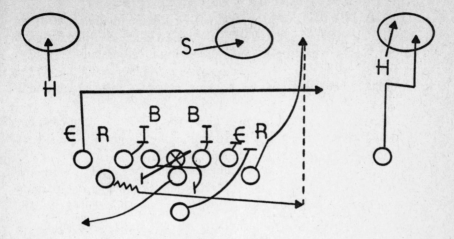

Diagram 12-19

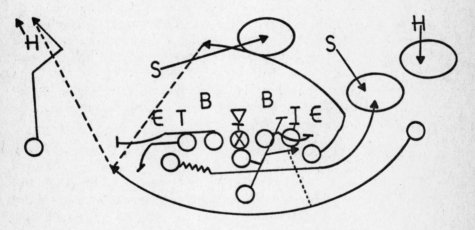

Diagram 12-20

split end runs a flag pattern off an initial post fake and is the primary receiver. As a secondary receiver the backside halfback releases and works
across the middle opposite the rotational movement of the middle safety.
The ball carrier receives the pitch and gains some depth. He looks first for
the split end on the flag pattern and then the backside halfback as the secondary receiver over the middle.

SCREEN PASSES

Screen passes from the Double Slot formation are used most effectively in the following situations:

1) Screens can be used to beat defensive alignments that control the width and depth of the field. The basic Double Slot formation is designed to accomplish this by its initial alignment. Defenses that play "prevent" type secondaries are vulnerable to the screen pass as the "underneath" zones develop with considerable depth.

2) Screens can be successfully used against the opposite of category #1. That is, against defenses that pressure the passing game with blitzes and various other stunts.

3) Screens can be used as an element of surprise, utilized when the defense is least expecting it. For example, run a screen pass on first down at around midfield or just into an opponents territory.

In all screen passes the offensive line and quarterback must be good actors. Offensive linemen must simulate dropback pass blocking, making the defense think that a pass play is developing that is directing the ball deep into the secondary. Individual linemen must allow the individual defender to think that he has beaten the offensive blocker. The offensive lineman then slides away from the defender and forms a screen for the ball carrier. As for the quarterback he must fake completely his initial ball action before delivery of the ball into the screen area.

Examples of three screen pass categories will be presented. These classifications include dropback action, sprint out and various screens as they are worked from play actions.

DROPBACK SCREENS

Diagram 12-21 illustrates a dropback action screen thrown to the fullback. This screen is thrown to the tight end side and is named in the huddle as "Dropback Fullback Screen Strong." The defense is a 5-2 with a "corner" rotation into the tight end side of the formation. Key techniques are as follows:

Offensive line:
>> **Playside Guard**—Pass block. Release. Block the middle defender.
>> **Playside Tackle**—Pass block. Release. Block the "corner force" or the outside defender.
>> **Center**—Pass block. Release. Peel back on the defensive pursuit from the inside.

> **Fullback**—Set up to pass block to the strong side (tight end side). Allow penetration and slide 3 yards outside the tight end looking for the ball.

Quarterback—Use a 7 yard drop. React to pressure by dropping still deeper (to 9 yards). Pass the ball to the fullback.

Tight end—On the playside, release and block the defender covering the deep outside 1/3.

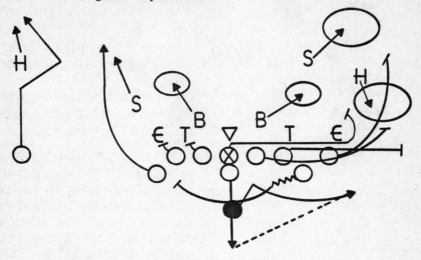

Diagram 12-21

Another dropback screen is shown in diagram 12-22, this time to a halfback on the strong side of the offensive formation. The primary receiver is the backside halfback that goes in "fly" motion sets to pass

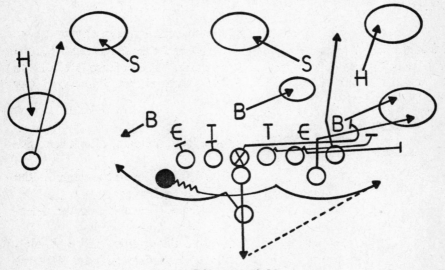

Diagram 12-22

block and reacts the same as the fullback did on the previous screen play. The halfback actually executes his "cup" protection assignment and then slides out into the screen area. The halfback technique is to set up, read the rush and then slide to a position 3 yards outside the tight end's original position. The fullback also sets up to execute "cup" protection, but then "flare controls" the backside. A 4-3 defense is being attacked. The defensive secondary is rotating the corner to the weak side (split end side) of the offensive formation as dropback pass action shows.

The play schemes illustrated in diagrams 12-21 and 12-22 are classified as "delay" type screens. In these situations the play action takes a considerable amount of time in which to develop. Also run off dropback pass action are "quick screens," an example of which is shown in diagram 12-23. When running the quick screen, the offensive linemen release immediately. There is no delay for the fullback or halfback depending upon the backfield action. The quarterback retreats quickly and sets up as soon as possible. In diagram 12-23 the quick screen to the fullback is run at a 4-4 defense. The secondary and linebackers have adjusted to the 2 split end formation. "Motion" is used by the halfback with the defensive secondary switching to man-to-man coverage. The playside linemen release quickly and block the same assignments as for the regular delay type screens. This screen can also be considered as a "weak" pass in that it is directed away from the "motion" in a 2 split end formation. The huddle call would be made as follows: "Motion Right Fullback Quick Screen Left."

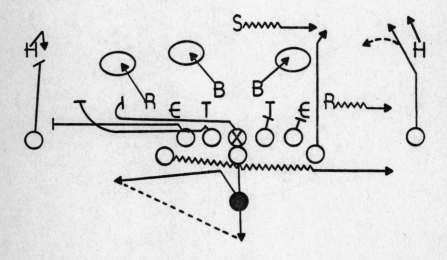

Diagram 12-23

Diagram 12-24 shows a "double screen" that develops also off the dropback pass action. The offensive line releases and establishes screens to both sides of the formation. Both the offensive backs block for 2 counts (delay type screen) and then slide into their areas. The strategy behind the "double screen" is to throw to one of the backs if the other is covered. In 12-24 the offense is attacking a 4-3 defense. The center drive blocks the middle linebacker and then slides toward the strong side (tight end side) of the formation.

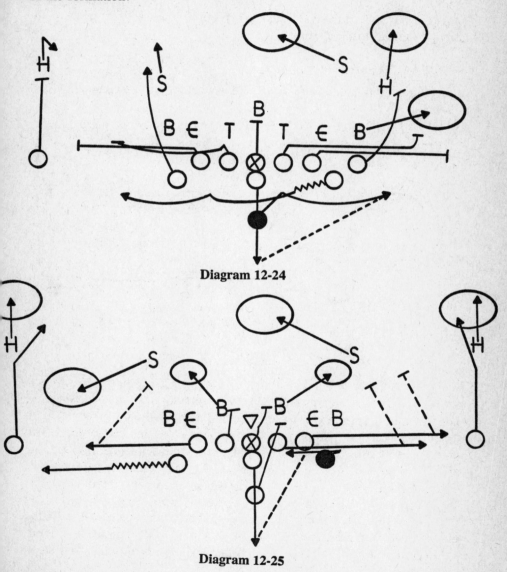

Diagram 12-24

Diagram 12-25

A very effective middle screen is illustrated in diagram 12-25. In this play the stationary halfback is the primary receiver. The halfback must sit and fake a pass block on the defensive end for two counts before sliding to the middle behind the blocking wall. All offensive linemen with the exception of the left guard and center pull directly towards the sidelines. After the pass is thrown, these linemen flow back to the inside and assist with the blocking downfield. "Jet" motion is used to the backside away from the intended screen. The fullback fills and blocks over the position of the right guard. The quarterback retreats quickly and throws the ball to the halfback.

QUICK SCREENS

Plays of this category are based on sprint out pass action. Quick

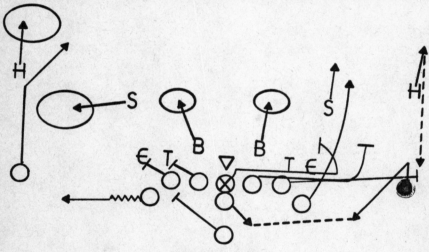

Diagram 12-26

screens are illustrated in diagrams 12-26 and 12-27. In 12-26 a quick screen to the wide receiver is shown. In this situation the playside linemen release quickly sprinting to the outside and then downfield to block a path for the ball carrier. The playside halfback releases and clears deep. The split end drives off for three steps, plants and comes back behind the line to receive the ball from the quarterback. The key block is the offensive tackle, he must block the defensive halfback (or corner contain defender) rotating forward. "Jet" motion develops away from the playside, forcing the defense to rotate its coverage that way. The fullback also moves in the direction of the motion, enhancing the flow read to the defensive secondary. As the snap is taken, the quarterback sprints out for two steps towards the playside. He sets up quickly and throws the ball to the wide receiver.

Full sprint action is shown in diagram 12-27. Here the quarterback sprints out in the direction of motion. He then sets up and throws the ball back to the stationary halfback behind a screen of blockers. "Jet" motion to the sprint out side results in invert coverage from the defensive secondary. The wide receiver to the screen side runs off the defender responsible for the deep outside 1/3 to his side. Because of the quick action of the sprint out pass, the playside offensive linemen do not delay their release into the screen. The stationary halfback (primary receiver) delays at the line, and turns back towards the play action looking for the ball from the quarterback. A great deal of the success of this play depends upon the drop of the outside linebackers to the playside. If the defender is staying

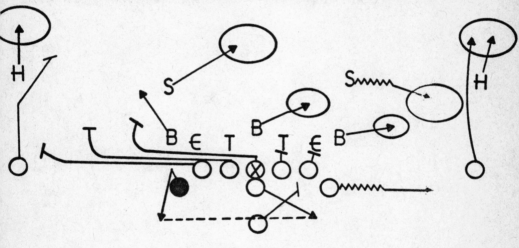

Diagram 12-27

close to the line, then one of the screen blockers must take him to keep the defender off the intended receiver.

PLAY ACTION SCREENS

An example of a play action screen is shown in diagram 12-28. Here Veer action is run into the split end side of the formation with a screen designed to go to the tight end aligned to the opposite side. After a good ride fake to the fullback, the quarterback drops back and looks to throw to the tight end in behind the developing screen. The technique for the tight end is to use an outside release and then peel back behind the line of scrimmage, turning inside to look for the ball from the quarterback. Offensive linemen block for 2 counts (allowing for a good Veer fake) and then slide to the outside, executing their basic screen assignments. To the Veer side, the linemen fire out to place maximum effect on the running fake.

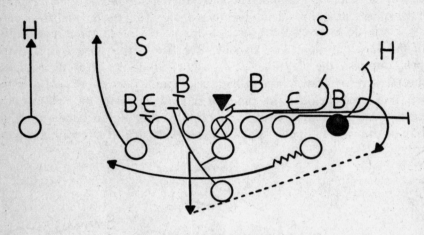

Diagram 12-28

Index

A

"A" block, 36–37
  and straight option, 79
Alignments, defensive, 26–31
"Arc" block, 40

B

Backfield blocking, 146
Belly action passes, 200–201 (see also "Play action and screen passes . . . .")
Belly Counter, 94–97 (see also "Belly series. . . .")
Belly Handback Trap, 93–94
Belly Option, 92–93
Belly series, coaching, 89–101
  Belly Counter, 94–97
    and "jet" motion, 96–97
    techniques, special, 94–95
  Belly Handback Trap, 93–94
  Belly Option, 92–93
  Counter Tackle Trap, 97–100
    assignments and techniques, 97–98
    vs. 4–4 defense, 99–100
  naming plays, 101
  Outside Belly, 90–92
    assignments, 90–91
    blocking adjustments, 91–92
    "jet" motion, 91
Blocking adjustments for Triple Option, 46
  "loop" blocking scheme, 46
Blocking calls for Double Option, 41–43
  "lead" technique, 43
  "X" call, 42

Blocking schemes in Veer series, 35–38
Bootleg by Quarterback, 112–113
Bootleg Sweep, 75–76 (see also "Buck series")
Bootlegs, 206–208 (see also "Play action and screen passes. . . .")
Buck action bootleg left 6 fullback flat, 207–208
Buck action O passes, 201–202 (see also "Play action and screen passes. . . .")
Buck series, 61–76
  Bootleg Sweep, 75–76
  Fullback Buck Drive, 62–65
    assignments, 62–64
    coaching points, 64–65
    "35 Buck Dive," 65
  Fullback Buck Trap, 65–68
    assignments and techniques, 65–68
    influence technique, 66
    naming, 68
  naming, 76
  Off-Tackle, 68–72
    assignments, 68–71
    coaching points, 71–72
  Sweep, 72–75
    coaching points, 74–75
    techniques, 73–74
Buck sweep right halfback pass, 209–210

C

"Combo" blocking scheme, 35–36
Complementary running plays, coaching, 103–115
  Bootleg by Quarterback, 112–113
  End Around, 103–108
    assignments and techniques, 104–105

219

Complementary running plans, (cont.)
    End Around, (cont.)
        coaching points, 107–108
        Fullback Option action, 106
        and "jet" motion, 106–107
    naming plays, 115
    Power Sweep, 111–112
        assignment and techniques, 111–112
        Halfback Reverse, 113–115 (see also
            "Halfback Reverse. . . .")
    Tight End Sweep, 108–111
        coaching points, 109–110
        at different defensive fronts, 110–111
Complementary Veer plays, coaching, 49–59
    end option, 57–59
        techniques, 58–59
    Halfback Slant, 49–57
        assignments and techniques, 50–53
        "G" blocking assignment, 53–54
        summary of blocking calls, 54
        with triple blocking, 54–57
Counter Tackle Trap, 97–100 (see also "Belly
    series. . . .")
"Cup" blocking with "fly" motion, 150–151
"Cup" protection, 144–145, 149

                            D

Defense, creating problems for, 15–16
Defensive alignments, chart of, 26–31
"Delay" type screens, 214
Development of play-calling system, 15–31
    defense, problems for, 15–16
    double slot, what it is, 15–16
    formations, 16–20
        seven-yard boundary, reason for, 17
        standard, 16–17
        "Tight Slot Right" or "Tight Slot Left,"
            18–19
    huddle, 23–24
    line blocking rules, 26–31
    motion types, 20–23
        "fly," 23
        "jet," 22
        "motion," 20–21
        "twins" formation, 22
    naming play, 24–26
Double Option, 38–43
    assignments and techniques, 40–41
    blocking calls and adjustments, special,
        41–43
        "lead" technique, 43

Double Option, (cont.)
    "X" call, 42
    quarterback, special techniques for, 41
Double slot, definition of, 15–16
    formation, standard, 16–17
Dropback, 140–141
Dropback pass game, coaching, 171–188
    flare control, 175–178
    strong side, 171–175
        "flare read," 172
        fly dropback 51 cup, 173–174
        jet dropback 49, 172–173
        jet dropback 59, 174–175
        two-man patterns, 171–172
    three-man patterns, 178–183
        "hot receiver," 179–180
        motion dropback 202, 180–181
        motion dropback 502 "hot," 182–183
        motion dropback 528, 181–182
    weak side, 183–188
        attacking with single receiver, 184–185
        jet right dropback weak 21 flare control,
            186
        jet right dropback weak 51 FB swing,
            187–188
        jet right dropback weak 62 FB flat, 188
        three-man patterns, 186
        weak side pass attack 2 receivers, 185–186
Dropback protection, 144–145
Dropback screens, 212–216

                            E

End Around, 103–108 (see also "Complemen-
    tary running plays. . . .")
End around pass, 210–211
End option, 57–59
    techniques, 58–59

                            F

"Feathering" defender, quarterback's special
        technique for, 41
Flare control, 175–178
"Flare read," 172
Fly dropback 51 cup, 173–174
"Fly" motion, 23
"Fly" motion, Fullback Option and, 83–84
Fly right sprint right 21 fullback flat, 159–160
Fly right sprint right 49, 156
Fly right spring right 49 fullback circle, 162–
    163

Fly right sprintback right 1, 164–165
Formations, 16–20
4 Deep defense, 127–129, 130
4-4 defense, Counter Tackle Trap vs., 99–100
Fullback Buck Dive, 62–65 (see also "Buck series")
Fullback Buck Trap, 65–68 (see also "Buck series")
Fullback option, 79–88 (see also "Option plays. . . .")
Fullback option action "motion" right 798, 204–205
Fullback Veer series, 33–47 (see also " Veer series. . . .")

G

"G" blocking assignment against Slant, 53–54
in Outside Belly, 92

H

Halfback option pass right, 209
Halfback Reverse of Power Sweep, 113–115
coaching points, 114–115
techniques, basic, 114
Halfback Slant, 49–57
assignments and techniques, 50–53
"G" blocking assignments, 53–54
summary of blocking calls, 54
with triple blocking, 54–57
Hand-off key, 43–47 (see also "Triple Option")
Hinge blocking, 143–144
"Hot receiver," 179–180
Huddle alignment, 23–24

I

Influence technique in Fullback Buck Trap, 66

J

Jet dropback 49, 172–173
Jet dropback 59, 174–175
Jet left sprint right 2, 154–155
Jet left sprint right 22, 160–161
Jet left sprint right 95 pick, 161–162
"Jet" motion, 22

and Belly Counter, 96–97
in End Around, 106–107
with Fullback Option, 82–88
and Outside Belly, 91
Jet right dropback weal 21 flare control, 186
Jet right dropback weak 51 FB swing, 187–188
Jet right dropback weak 62 FB flat, 188
Jet right fullback option left 68, 205–206
Jet right sprint right 4, 155–156
Jet right sprint right 81, 156–158
Jet right sprint right 85, 158
Jet right sprintback right 49, 166–167
Jet right sprintback right 59, 165–166

L

Lead action passes, 202–206 (see also "Play action and screen passes. . . .")
"Lead" technique, 43
Line blocking rules. 26–31
"Loop" blocking, 46, 79

M

Man-to-man combinations 4 Deep, 131–132
"Max," meaning of, 147–148
Motion dropback 202, 180–181
Motion dropback 502 "hot," 182–183
Motion dropback 528, 181–182
Motion right sprint right 945, 158–159
Motion types, 20–23
"fly," 23
"jet," 22
"motion," 20–21
"twins" formation, 22

N

Number descriptions in plays, 25

O

Off-Tackle, 68–72 (see also "Buck series")
Option plays, special, 77–88
Fullback Option, 79–88
assignments, 79–82
and "fly" motion, 83–84
with "jet" motion, 82–88

Option plays, (cont.)
  naming plays, 88
  straight option, 77–79
    assignments, 77–78
    against defensive alignment variations, 79
Outside Belly, 90–92 (see also "Belly
    series. . . .")

                              P

Pass actions, establishing, 137–152
  basic, 137–141
    dropback, 140–141
    rollout, 137–139
    sprint out, 139
  blocking assignments and techniques, 142–
      151
    backfield assignments for dropback protec-
        tion, 148–149
    backfield blocking assignments, 146
    "cup" blocking with "fly" motion, 150–
        151
    "cup" protection, 144–145, 149
    dropback protection, 144–145
    fullback, techniques for, 147–148
    halfbacks, assignments for, 149–151
    hinge blocking, 143–144
    "Max," meaning of, 147–148
    sprint and rollout protection assignments,
        142–143
    team protection techniques, 151–152
Pass play calling, developing, 117–123
  naming actions and patterns, 123
  patterns, basic, for receivers, 118–122
  release techniques by receivers, 117–118
Play action and screen passes, coaching, 189–
    218
  advantages, 189–190
  belly action passes, 200–201
    belly right action 52, 201
  bootlegs, 206–208
    buck action bootleg left 6 fullback flat,
        207–208
    power sweep bootleg left 6 tight end drag,
        206–207
    Veer right action bootleg left 6 halfback
        drag, 208
  buck action passes, 201–202
    buck action right 45, 201–202
  lead action passes, 202–206
    fullback option action "motion" right 798,
        204–205

Play action and screen passes (cont.)
    jet right fullback option left 68, 205–206
    straight option action right 28, 203
  screen passes, 211–218
    "delay" type, 214
    "double screen," 215
    dropback screens, 212–216
    play action, 217–218
    quick screens, 216–217
    uses of, 212
  slant action passes, 197–200
    points, key, 197–198
    slant right action 22, 198–199
    slant right action 87 tight end drag,
        199–200
    slant right action 89, 200
  special passes, 208–211
    buck sweep right halfback pass, 209–210
    end around pass, 210–211
    halfback option pass right, 209
    power sweep right halfback pass, 210
  throwback strategy with Veer action pass,
      196–197
  Veer action passes, 190–197
    points, key, 190
    techniques, individual, 191–192
    Veer right action 28, 192–193
    Veer right action 49, 193–195
    Veer right action 59 pick, 195–196
Power Sweep, 111–112 (see also "Complemen-
    tary running. . . .")
Power sweep bootleg left 6 tight end drag,
    206–207
Power sweep right halfback pass, 210

                              Q

Quarterback, special techniques for in Double
    Option, 41
Quarterbacks, special techniques for in Triple
    Option, 45–46
Quarterback Sweep, 75–76 (see also "Buck
    series")
Quick screens, 216–217

                              R

Receivers, release techniques by, 117–118
  pass patterns, basic, 118–122
Release techniques by receivers, 117–118

Rollout, 137–139
  semi-roll technique, 137–139

S

Screen passes, 211–218 (see also "Play action
    and screen passes. . . .")
Secondary coverages, 124–135
  combinations, 130–131
  man-to-man combinations 4 Deep, 131–132
  man-to-man coverages, 129–132
    3 Deep, 129–130
    4 Deep, 130
  motion, secondary adjustments to, 133–135
  zone coverages, 124–129
    3 Deep, 124–126
    4 Deep, 127–129
Semi-roll technique, 137–139
Semi-sprint technique, 139
Slant, 49–57
  assignments and techniques, 50–53
  "G" blocking assignment, 53–54
  summary of blocking calls, 54
  with triple blocking, 54–57
Slant action passes, 197–201 (see also "Play
    action and screen passes. . . .")
"Slant read" play, 56
Sprint out, 139
  semi-sprint technique, 139
Sprint out pass game, coaching, 153–169
  one-man patterns, 154–156
    jet left sprint right 2, 154–155
    jet right sprint right 4, 155–156
  semi-sprint action, 160–163
    fly right sprint right 49 fullback circle,
      162–163
    jet left sprint right 22, 160–161
    jet left sprint right 95 pick, 161–162
  three-man combinations, 158–160
    fly right sprint right 21 fullback flat,
      159–160
    motion right sprint right 945, 158–159
  throwback action against 4-deep secondaries,
      167–169
    sprintback right 22, 168–169
    sprintback right 49, 168
  throwback strategy, 163–167
    fly right sprintback right 1, 164–165
    jet right sprintback right 49, 166–167
    jet right sprintback right 59, 165–166
  two-man patterns, 156–158
    fly right sprint right 49, 156

Sprint out pass game, (cont.)
  two-man patterns, (cont.)
    jet right sprint right 81, 156–158
    jet right sprint right 85, 158
Sprint and rollout protection assignments, 142–
    143
Sprintback 49 right 49, 168
Sprintback right 22, 168–169
"Step" block, 36–37
Straight option, 77–79 (see also "Option
    plays. . . .")
Straight option action right 28, 203

T

Tackle Trap, 97–100 (see also "Belly
    series. . . .")
"35 Buck Dive," 65 (see also "Buck Series")
3 Deep defenses, 124–126, 129–130
Tight End Sweep, 108–111 (see also "Com-
    plementary running plays. . . .")
Triple Option, 43–47
  assignments and techniques, 44–46
  blocking adjustments and variations, 47
  "loop" scheme, 47
  quarterbacks, special techniques for, 45–46
Triple Option blocking pattern, Slant play and,
    54–57
"Twins" formation, 22

V

Veer action passes, 190–197 (see also "Play
    action and screen passes. . . .")
Veer right action bootleg left 6 halfback drag,
    208
Veer series, coaching, 33–47
  assignments and techniques, 35
  blocking calls, 35–38
  Double Option, 38–43
    assignments and techniques, 40–41
    blocking calls and adjustments, special,
      41–43 (see also "Double Option")
    quarterback, special techniques for, 41
  extensions, 49–59 (see also "Complementary
    Veer plays. . . .")
  hand-off key, 43–47 (see also "Triple Op-
    tion")
  Triple Option, 43–47
    assignments and techniques, 44–46
    blocking adjustments, 47 (see also "Triple
      Option")

Veer Series, (*cont.*)
  Triple Option, (*cont.*)
    quarterbacks, special techniques for, 45–46
  what it is, 33–34

W

Word descriptions in plays, 25

X

"X" blocking call, 42